For Tamara —
Thanks so much
for your professional
talent and your
friendship!
Love,
Diana

Chris

The Illustration of Plants and Gardens
1500–1850

Victoria and Albert Museum

The Illustration of
Plants & Gardens
1500~1850
Vera Kaden

Fig. 55

224.

SMINUM SEMPER VIRENS AMERICANUM

Munting: Naauwkeurige Beschrijving.

Contents

Volckamer: Nürnbergische Hesperides.

Acknowledgements

My very special thanks go to Martin Bladon, who took the photographs. Without his highly professional work and helpful cooperation this book could never have been published. I should also like to express my thanks to colleagues in the Museum who read the typescript and who gave me encouragement.

Volckamer: Nürnbergische Hesperides.

Introduction

The library of the Victoria and Albert Museum has in its collection a number of fine illustrated botanical works. They cover nearly five hundred years and are examples of some of the best processes of European book production and illustration of their time. This is the reason for their being in a Museum devoted to the decorative arts and in a Library devoted to art history and the art of the book. Essentially they were not acquired for their botanical interest but for their aesthetic appeal, though in the best examples it is difficult to separate the two.

As the books illustrate plants and flowers grown in gardens, an attempt has been made to relate the history of styles of gardening to the history of herbals and flower books. To achieve this the reader will to some extent be moved backwards and forwards in time. This may be no bad thing since it can serve as a reminder that garden fashions did not move in strict chronological order – enclosed, formal, landscape – but that they changed gradually, one style merging and overlapping with another, two styles existing side by side in the same way as they did in the books that the gardens and flowers gave rise to.

As this is in no way a comprehensive bibliography of the illustrated books in the Library, a selection has had to be made. This has meant that, sadly, many fine books in the collection have had to be excluded. The choice has been a personal and subjective one, but I have tried to include the best or those which were the most important. The period covered by this book ends in the mid-nineteenth century – a time which saw the end of the excellence of illustrated botanical works. There are exceptions, of course, but after about 1860 little was produced to match the masterpieces of the previous centuries.

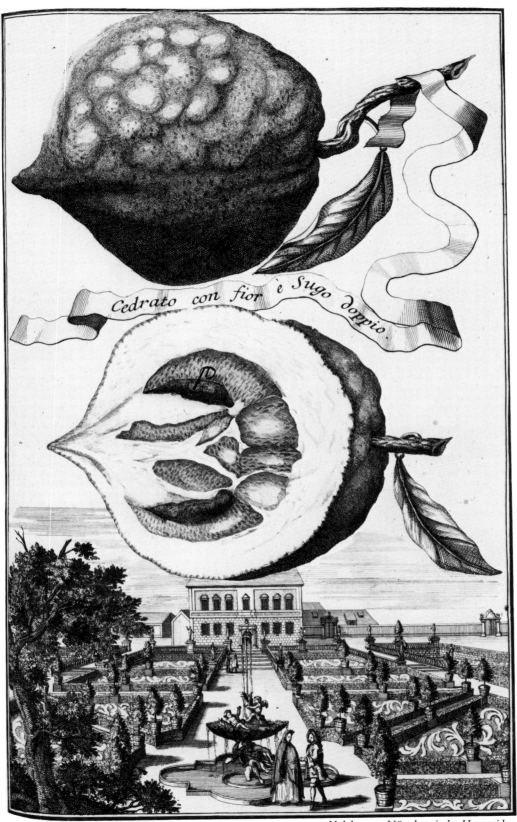

Cedrato con fior è Sugo doppio

Volckamer: Nürnbergische Hesperides.

Colombina: Il Bomprovifaccia.

The physician's garden & his herbal

With the end of feudal strife, the discovery of the New World and the invention of printing, a new era was clearly beginning as the fifteenth century drew to its close. For the garden historian, the Tudor period was the start of a more precise state of knowledge. The end of feudal strife brought greater peace and leisure; the discovery of the New World meant the introduction of new plants; and the invention of printing meant the appearance of the first printed herbals.

Our knowledge now starts to be based upon the printed word and less on conjecture. Until this time our ideas about the medieval garden were based on the work of painters, poets, illuminators or the weavers of tapestries. From them we know that the garden of the Middle Ages was enclosed, surrounded by walls or a woven fence or hedge, that it contained a flowering mead, a mound, a turfed seat, rectangular beds of flowers and herbs, gravelled paths, and that it often contained an arbour and a fountain. Despite the evident delight that was taken in gardens and flowers at this time, almost everything that grew in a garden was basically for use rather than exclusively for pleasure: apart from the vegetables and herbs, even the rose, the violet, the primrose, the lilies or the gladioli, as well as many others, all had some medicinal or culinary use.

At this time – and until the seventeenth century – medicine and botany were two inseparable areas of knowledge. The early herbals were generally compiled by physicians, herbalists or apothecaries who grew in their gardens the plants about which they wrote in order to be able to prepare the medicines that they required.

At the end of the fifteenth century, plants and flowers are depicted with such delicacy, sophistication and realism in paintings or in the borders of illuminated manuscripts that it comes as something of a shock to turn from these to the woodcut illustrations of the early printed herbals. Here the plants are depicted in a manner both lively and vigorous, but at the same time crude and strikingly lacking in realism. There were a number of reasons for this. Printing was a new medium and detailed woodcuts were difficult to achieve. The illustrations were printed with the text and not on a separate leaf. Early woodcut illustrations in all books tended to be used in a more diagrammatic way, almost more to divide the text than to give an accurate image. Blame for the absence of realism, however, could also be put on the lack of original work on the part of the illustrators. The text of many of the early herbals was based on a work of the first century, *De Materia Medica* by Dioscorides. This remained the most important influence on herbals from the first to the seventeenth century. It was frequently copied and illustrators tended to copy the illustrations from one version to the next, rather than turn to the plants themselves.

In 1485 the German *Herbarius* was printed containing original woodcuts done from nature. Some fifteen years later the *Ortus Sanitatis* (pls. 1, 4) was printed and many of its woodcuts were taken from the *Herbarius* and frequently distorted in copying. This use of woodcuts from earlier works was a common practice and, as a result, illustrations became increasingly detached from reality as each version was more misunderstood and changed. Difficulties of identification must often have presented themselves for readers of early herbals. Apart from the *Grete Herbal*, 1526 (pl. 3), which was the first illustrated English publication of its kind, very few noteworthy herbals were published at the start of the sixteenth century until we come to the appearance of Otto Brunfels's *Herbarum Vivae Eicones* (pls. 5, 6) in three volumes between 1530 and 1536. With this work a new era of botanical illustration began. The merit of this *Herbarum* rests not upon the text, which was based on the work of Italian herbalists, but on the woodcuts, which were made from drawings by Hans Weiditz, an associate, perhaps a pupil, of Dürer. Weiditz worked from nature and not from other men's illustrations and consequently achieved greater accuracy as well as greater beauty than any of his predecessors.

Another possible cause for the crudity of early botanical illustrations may have been the use of so many 'middlemen'. The author employed an artist. He in his turn may have employed someone to copy the drawing on to the block and yet another may have done the actual

Fuchs: De Historia Stirpium.

Fuchs: De Historia Stirpium.

cutting of the wood block. With so many people involved in the production of an illustration, much depended on their technical ability and their integrity as artists. One author who was extremely fortunate in the artistic ability of those involved in his illustrations was Leonard Fuchs who, in 1542, published his *De Historia Stirpium*, in which his acknowledgment of his artists was more generous than that which Brunfels had given Weiditz. Albrecht Meyer, the artist, Heinrich Füllmaurer, who copied the drawings on to the wood, and Veit Rudolf Speckle, the engraver, are all portrayed at the end of the herbal (pls. 7, 8). The illustrations combined realism, accuracy and elegance, with the latter predominating. The illustrations in Fuchs's work are more generously displayed on the page than they are in Brunfels's *Herbarum* though the actual lines are thinner and there is not the texture of the plant shown by Weiditz. As was so often the case at this time, the illustrations were probably intended for hand-colouring by the owner of the book.

One of the penalties of success was the repeated use and pirating of any plates and designs that had proved popular. Fuchs's plates continued to be used for herbals by other authors for many years, even centuries, to come. Few herbals published in the sixteenth century, however, were to compare in quality with either of these two works.

In 1544 Pietro Andrea Matthiolus, a physician from Siena, published his commentary on Dioscorides, *Commentarii in sex libros Pedacii Dioscoridis*. Matthiolus was given manuscript copies of the work of Dioscorides by Ogier Ghiselin Busbecq, the ambassador of the Emperor Ferdinand I at the court of Sultan Suleiman the Magnificent. (Busbecq was also responsible for the introduction of a number of new plants, including the tulip, to northern Europe.) The first edition of Matthiolus's commentary was unillustrated. It was extremely popular and subsequently appeared in many illustrated editions in a number of languages. The woodcuts here create a totally different effect from those in the two preceding works, being more dense and designed to fit the block, where possible covering it entirely (pls. 9, 10) and using more shading than can be found in Fuchs's work. Nevertheless, the illustrations are not always entirely accurate as the drawings were based on dried plants and not on fresh ones.

Although successful illustrations resulted in pirating and copying of plates, in one instance the use of the same illustrations for the works of three different authors was done entirely with their approval. Rembert Dodoens, Charles de l'Ecluse (Carolus Clusius) and Matthias de l'Obel (Lobelius) were three great botanists of Flanders and France. All three had their work published in Antwerp by Christophe Plantin and illustrated by blocks belonging to the printer. The result was that the same illustration frequently appeared in the works of all three authors (pls. 11, 12). The majority of the actual drawings from which the blocks were made were drawn from nature by Pierre van der Borcht (c.1540–1608), who worked for Plantin and who was responsible for the illustrations of all botanical works, as well as others, printed by Plantin. Many of the botanical blocks used by the latter still exist today in the Plantin-Moretus Museum in Antwerp.

Other herbals, such as those of William Turner and John Gerard, mostly used illustrations previously used by other authors. William Turner's *A New Herball* (published in three parts in 1551, 1562 and 1568) was the first based on a more scientific approach, though the woodcut illustrations are largely copied from Fuchs. John Gerard's *Herball* was published by John Norton in 1597 and contained only some sixteen original woodcuts, the remainder being taken from other earlier works. Norton acquired some of the woodblocks from the press of Nicolaus Bassaeus in Frankfurt, where they had been used to illustrate a herbal, *Eicones Plantarum*, published in 1590 by Jacob Dietrich or Tabernaemontanus. An enlarged and amended edition of Gerard's *Herball* was prepared by Thomas Johnson in 1633 and published by John Norton's successors. This time the woodblocks for the illustrations came from Christophe Plantin in Antwerp, where they had been used for the works of Dodoens, Clusius and Lobelius. Both editions of Gerard's work have remarkably fine title-pages. The title-page of the 1597 edition is particularly attractive and is an early example of one made from an engraving on copper rather than wood (pl. 13). It was designed and engraved by William Rogers, one of the first English exponents of copper-plate engraving, an art that was not practised in England before about 1540, though on the Continent it had been used for nearly a century.

Hyll: The Profitable Arte of Gardening.

Meanwhile, as herbals were coming over from the presses of Europe, gardens in England were changing. In the Tudor period the garden had developed from a simple enclosure of mound, grass, flowers and herb garden situated close to the house to a more complex series of enclosures. William Lawson's plan (pl. 15) charmingly covers all the essentials of the well-appointed garden of the time. His house has a moat and a river, but the enclosure could be achieved by walls, thorn hedges, fences or banks. There would often have been alleys of pleached trees, with herbs growing under foot and trellised walks. Each little garden within the area marked off by walls would be self-contained. Near the house would be a terrace. Knots were important. These were square beds in which low shrubs – mostly box, rosemary or lavender – grew in intricate patterns. In some cases the shrubs would enclose flowerbeds. Later, flowers were considered too messy and were replaced by coloured sands. There were many other orna-ments, topiary and fountains. The fountains had a practical purpose and were consequently mostly to be found in the centre of the garden to facilitate watering. In addition to their usefulness, they were dec-orative and provided a variety of practical jokes (pl. 14).

Richer owners had bowling greens and tennis courts, summerhouses and galleries covered by trellises over which plants were trained to grow. Flowers, vegetables and herbs grew in a separate area. The beds were frequently raised and edged or enclosed by trellises or low railings.

At this time the Renaissance was in full flower in Italy, but only little influence was felt in England. The effect was more on architecture than on gardens, which showed some Italianate features, but which could not be described as Italian gardens.

Even the great royal gardens retained a specifically English quality. Hampton Court, Nonsuch, Theobalds, however splendid they may have been, were not Renaissance gardens in the Italian sense. Even Francis Bacon, admittedly not first and foremost a gardener, makes interesting observations on the taste in gardens of his time in his essay 'On Gardens'. He advocates standard Tudor features, such as a lawn near the house, an avenue of trees in the centre and shady walks on either side. He prefers green grass to parterres, and of knot beds filled with coloured earths he says they 'be but toys; you may see as good sights many times in tarts.' The main garden in the middle of the estate should be square, surrounded by a hedge with arches set up on a bank. Topiary is out. 'I do not like images cut out in juniper or other gardenstuffe, they be for children.' There should be trees of all kinds, including fruit trees. Walks should have mounds at the end and there should be fountains but not pools. 'Pools marr all,

Lawson: A New Orchard and Garden.

and make the Garden unwholesome and full of Flies and Frogs.' The third area that Bacon advocates for the ideal garden is the heath: 'a natural Wildness.'

Lonicer: Kreuterbuch.

Falda: *Li Giardini di Roma*.

The patterned gardens of Italy and France

Italian gardens in the early Middle Ages had been devoted chiefly to the cultivation of herbs and flowers for medicine and for cooking. Also, as in northern Europe, the Crusades had led to the introduction of new plants. In Sicily, however, the greater influences of Byzantium and Islam made themselves felt not only through the introduction of plants previously unknown – including, probably, the citrus fruit – and the increasing emphasis on the importance of water as a feature of gardens, but also through the whole concept of gardens for pleasure. Whereas northern castles remained fortresses, in Italy the villa or pleasure palace existed as early as the fourteenth century.

Leon Battista Alberti, the poet, scholar, art theorist and architect, is the first important writer on the design of gardens in the early Renaissance. He favoured a garden situated on a slope so that more stress is laid on the prospect than on the safety of an enclosed garden. While there were still enclosed gardens within gardens (*giardini segreti*) one of the three most important ideals in garden design at this time is the opening out of the garden so that the eye may take in the world beyond. The other two basic ideals were that the house and garden were to be considered as a single entity, the garden as an extension of the house, and that both were to create an atmosphere of welcome.

With the election in 1503 of Pope Julius II, the great patron of the arts, the architect Donato Bramante was commissioned to devise some means of linking the Pope's Villa Belvedere with the Vatican. Bramante found a solution which was to have a vital effect on the Renaissance garden in Italy. The problem was solved by constructing a series of terraces linked by great stairs, ramps and balustrades, with a line of vision ending with a semi-circular loggia (pl. 17). Subsequent gardens, in Rome particularly, had a distinctly architectural character, with terrace walks, walls and stairs as prominent features. The architectural knowledge necessary for the construction of these features meant that landscape gardeners had to have a knowledge of architecture or that, conversely, architects had to be the designers of gardens. At the same time classical statues and monumental fountains adorned the gardens, despite the problems of supplying water to Rome. The importance of water in a garden had been an idea imported from Islam via Sicily, as we have seen. It was developed into great displays: cascades, water-stairways and a variety of water jests that provided entertainment by unexpectedly soaking the spectator. Grottoes, too, became popular. Their construction was facilitated by the great supporting walls of terraces and stairs.

Despite all these innovations, some of the old features remained: the *giardini segreti* were now the modern equivalent of the medieval enclosure, and it was here that most of the flowers were grown. Covered walks remained and so did clipped box hedges. There were parterres visible from the house: their designs were geometrical rather than of the flowing complexity we find later in France. There were evergreen trees or single well-placed trees such as pines and cypresses. Fruit, vegetables, herbs and most flowers were kept in a separate part of the garden.

Falda: Li Giardini di Roma.

The Renaissance garden had moved from the private garden of the Middle Ages to the public work of display and pleasure. Nevertheless, the ideal of the best of the Renaissance gardens was still one of moderation. The gardens of the villas in Rome tended to be more ostentatious than those in the country – yet none was so extravagant as that of the Villa d'Este at Tivoli with its fantastic water gardens.

Some of the best evidence we have of the great Roman gardens of this period is from the engravings (pl. 16) of Giovanni Batista Falda's *Giardini di Roma* (c.1670). We have as well the written evidence of John Evelyn, who visited Rome in 1644–5 and cast his professional eye over the gardens. It is interesting to read the one while looking at the engravings of the other. Of the Quirinal (pl. 18), Evelyn says:

> I went farther up the hill, to the Popes Palace at Monte Cavallo, where I now saw the Garden more exactly, and found it to be one of the most magnificent & Pleasant in Rome: I am told the Gardner

is annualy alow'd 2000 scudi for the keeping it: Here I observ'd the glorious hedges of myrtle above a mans height; others of Laurell, Oranges, nay of Ivy, & Juniper; the Close walkes and Rustic Grotto, and another admirable Crypta whereof the Lavor or Basin is of one vast intire Porphyrie, the fairest that ever I beheld, antique; Below this falls a plentifull Cascad of Water; the stepps of the Grott being all of rich Mosaique, as is also the roofe; Here are hydraulic Organs; a fish-pond in an ample bath.

Of the gardens of the Villa Medici (pl. 19) Evelyn says:

Descending into the Garden is a noble fountaine govern'd by a Mercury of brasse, and a little distance on the left hand, a Lodge [loggia] full of incomparable statues, amongst which the Sabines, antique & singularly rare: in the Arcado [gallery] neere this stand 24 statues of infinite price; and hard by a Mount planted with Cypresses, representing a Fortresse, with a goodly fountain in the middle: Here also is a row balustr'd with white marble, on which are erected divers statues and heads, covered over with the natural shrubs, Ivys & other perennial Greenes. . . . There is likewise in this Garden a faire Obelisque full of Hieroglyphics.

And of the gardens of the Villa Borghese:

This garden abounded with all sorts of delicious fruit, and Exotique simples: Fountaines of sundry inventions, Groves & small Rivulets of Water: There is also adjoyning to it a Vivarium for Estriges [ostriches], Peacoks, Swanns, Cranes, &c: and divers strange Beasts, Deare & hares: the Grotto is very rare, and represents among other devices artificial raines, & sundry shapes of Vessells, Flowers &c: which is effected by [changing] the heads of the Fountains: the Groves are of Cypresse and Lawrell, Pine, Myrtil, Olive &c: the 4 Sphinxes are very Antique and worthy [of] observation: to this is a Volary full of curious birds.

It is interesting how much the artificial features of the garden struck Evelyn as worthy of mention, and how many of them there seem to have been. Various items referred to by Evelyn in his description of the Quirinal and the Villa Medici are clearly visible in Falda's engravings.

By the latter half of the seventeenth century, some of the architectural features were not given so much importance. Natural woods came to

Falda: Li Giardini di Roma.

be considered necessary to emphasize the beauty of a garden. At the same time ornament increased and with it came grotesquerie and fantastic diversions, such as the water theatre and the artificial singing birds. By the start of the eighteenth century, Italian gardens, like those of most of Europe, came under the influence of the French style of gardening.

Lonicer: Kreuterbuch.

The French style of gardening at the time of Louis XIV – and particularly the work of André Le Nôtre, its principal and brilliant exponent – was the culmination of developments in taste and fashion in the preceding decades. France had had little time, energy or inclination to devote to gardens during the Hundred Years' War. It was a time when a small enclosed garden, growing herbs and edible plants very close to the castle walls, was the most ambitious form of gardening anyone could aspire to.

In France, the Italian style became absorbed and changed. It took the French longer than the Italians to create gardens that were not enclosed, just as it took them longer to abandon the fortress-like style of architecture for their houses. There was no concept of house and garden as a single entity, nor was there necessarily any architectural relationship between the different levels of the garden.

In 1495, before Bramante's work at the Vatican, Charles VIII of France marched into Italy. He was immensely impressed by all that he saw and returned to France with a number of Italian artists in his retinue. Among them was the Neapolitan Pacello da Mercogliano, whom Charles employed to improve the gardens at Amboise. Later, after the death of Charles, Mercogliano worked at Blois for Louis XII.

The ground at Fontainebleau was so marshy and damp that a great lake was made (pl. 20) and this made still surfaces of water in lakes, canals and moats fashionable, rather than water stairways, cascades or other forms of moving water popular in Italy. Whereas Italian gardens were built on slopes, French gardens tended to be on flatter ground. This meant that views of the world outside – when the walled-in garden finally became less fashionable – were more difficult to achieve. After the middle of the sixteenth century, and with the rebuilding of the Château d'Anet for Diane de Poitiers by Philibert de l'Orme, the French garden tended no longer to be quite separate from the house. Furthermore, we now see a movement towards a very regular ground plan, with a central path or drive forming an axis with the centre of the building, both in front and behind it. This meant that viewpoints could now be constructed and vistas controlled. Symmetry was one of the great innovations of French garden design.

It was at the Château d'Anet, too, that the other great French contribution to gardening was first displayed. What had been popular throughout Europe as a 'knot garden' was developed in France from a series of small patterned rectangles into a large parterre. Italy had parterres, but they were not as important to the design of a garden as they became in France and they had continued the designs of the original knot garden, whereas the designs of the French parterre became more flowing and much more elaborate. In France they were intended to be admired from above: usually from the upper rooms of a château or from a raised walk. The 'compartiments de broderie' designs were not only for gardens, but were also, as the name implies, for use by embroiderers.

Lonicer: Kreuterbuch.

Jacques Boyceau's *Traité du jardinage* (pl. 23), published in 1638, was one of the first theoretical dissertations on the principles of gardening by a practising gardener, and as such it was a vital forerunner to the work of Le Nôtre. Boyceau abolished the idea of a garden having four distinct parts (vegetable, flower, medicinal, fruit), which had been advocated earlier by Olivier de Serres in 1600. He recognized instead only two divisions: a utilitarian part and the *jardin de plaisir*. He emphasized the need for proportion and for symmetry combined with variety; and stressed the importance of avenues (*allées*), covered and uncovered, provided that they were not too long. He recommended, too, architectural fountains, balustrades, steps, and canal and other still water surfaces. Grottoes, already popular in France, were approved of. Boyceau published a large number of designs for parterres, including designs for the Tuileries, the Jardins de Luxembourg and Versailles.

France was now at the start of the *Grand Siècle* and the reign of Louis XIV, during which the great palace and gardens of Versailles were created.

Flowers and flower books in the seventeenth century

Gerard: The Herbal

It began to be more fashionable in the seventeenth century to grow flowers for their own sakes: for their beauty and not merely for their utility. In 1629, John Parkinson published his *Paradisi in Sole*, in which he speaks of 'my garden of pleasant and delightful flowers', and in which the first section is called 'The Ordering of the Garden of Pleasure'. Nevertheless, this is essentially a book in the old tradition – a gardening book which reflects the author's pleasure in flowers that are principally grown for use. Parkinson was an apothecary and herbalist who owned a garden in Long Acre in London. He divides the *Paradisi* into three parts – the flower garden, the kitchen garden and the orchard – and describes nearly one thousand plants. Many of these are illustrated by woodblock engravings but all too frequently copied from the work of others. The book is notable for the charm of its text rather than for its illustrations, though the title-page, engraved by Christopher Switzer, is an exception (pl. 24). Parkinson's *Theatrum Botanicum*, published in 1640, is a true herbal – one of the largest English herbals ever published.

As flowers came to be appreciated in their own right, there came a new form of flower book: the florilegium. Many of these works were not intended for publication and remained as manuscripts but, happily, some are available as books. The florilegium coincided with the new process of illustration by copper-plate engraving, which gradually replaced the woodcut in popularity. It had been in use in Europe as early as the fifteenth century, but was used for the illustration of flower books only from the seventeenth century. Once copper-plate engraving became accepted as an illustrative process it gradually almost ousted the woodcut and remained the only technique until the 'invention' of aquatint and lithography in the eighteenth century.

Florilegia contained little or no text. They were picture books depicting

Gerard: The Herbal

different kinds of flowers and aimed at giving pleasure to the garden lover, perhaps serving also as a guide to identification. Sometimes they were pictorial records of particular collections of flowers in specific gardens. Sometimes they were an expensive form of nurseryman's catalogue. They were also used as pattern books, chiefly for embroidery, but also for designs for ceramic or metalwork ornamentation.

Where the Renaissance garden had a parterre made not exclusively of shrubs or coloured stones, there were flowers. New flowers were being bred and many were being imported from other countries: from the Near East and the New World. Many of the flowers taken for granted by us today caused excitements in the late sixteenth century which would only be equalled in the latter half of the twentieth century if an astronaut were to return from space with an entirely new plant from another planet.

Parkinson had spoken of 'outlandish flowers' (as opposed to English): tulips came to Europe in the 1550s, fritillaries not long after; John Tradescant travelled to Russia, to North Africa and a number of European countries for Lord Salisbury, returning with new seeds and plants for the gardens at Hatfield; explorers came from the Americas, merchants from the Near East – and all, or nearly all, brought new plants.

Many of the florilegia depicted these new plants. The *Hortus Floridus* (1614) of Crispin de Passe, one of a family of Dutch engravers, was one of the earliest florilegia and contains very fine copper-plate engravings (pls. 25, 26). This book, published in Latin, Dutch, French and English, makes its first impact by its extreme simplicity. It is realistic and delicate, the delicacy being achieved through the use of line engraving which would not have been possible with a woodcut. The book is divided into sections corresponding to the seasons, and introducing each section is an engraving of a Dutch garden. True to the fashion of the time, the garden is symmetrically arranged with edged flower beds, a trellised gallery open to the garden, ornamentation of topiary, statues, balustrades and archways. Among the flowers are tulips, lilies, crown imperials, daffodils, hyacinths, narcissi, irises and peonies.

Another florilegium of about this time was Johann Theodore de Bry's *Florilegium Novum* (1612), which is also illustrated with copper-plate engravings (pls. 27, 28). The fine engraved title-page is the first architectural one I have chosen to illustrate this book. The engraved title-page was nothing new; it had been in existence since the early sixteenth century, and an architectural one which forms a doorway or arch for the reader to go through to enter the book, was first used in the 1550s. De Bry's title-page uses some of the architectural features of the well-appointed garden: the corinthian columns and the balustrade make the reader feel that he is viewing a particularly fine garden containing 'exoticks' (prickly pear and banana tree) from a shady arbour overgrown with other plants. Numerous editions of this book were published, one by de Bry's son-in-law, the engraver Matthäus Merian. Some of the plates in the book are taken from florilegia by other authors.

A florilegium relating to one specific garden was Basil Besler's huge *Hortus Eystettensis* (pls. 29, 30). Besler was a pharmacist in charge of the gardens belonging to Johann Konrad von Gemmingen, Prince Bishop of Eichstätt, near Nuremberg. It took Besler some sixteen years to complete the drawings of the plants in the Prince Bishop's garden, and the result is a monumental work containing elegant and accurate engravings by a number of different artists. Once again the title-page is an architectural one, more overtly so than that of de Bry and very much more baroque in style. It is a very fine engraving, but its massive weightiness belies the elegance of the botanical engravings that follow. The title-page bears the signature of Wolfgang Kilian of Augsburg, one of a whole dynasty of engravers and publishers. Kilian was also responsible for a number of the subsequent engravings in this work. Besler's portrait and arms are probably by the Würzburg engraver Johann Leypold, whose initials appear on other engravings such as the particularly graceful one of tulips (pl. 30).

Besler: Hortus Eystettensis.

In the seventeenth century the growing of citrus fruit became fashionable and a number of books on the subject were published. Giovanni Batista Ferrari's *Hesperides* (1646) contains many beautiful engravings after the work of some of Italy's leading artists, most notably the allegorical title-page is engraved by Johann Friedrich Greuter after a drawing by Pietro da Cortona, the great Italian painter and baroque architect (pl. 32). The engravings of the citrus fruits were made by Cornelis Bloemart (pl. 31). In the early eighteenth century Johann Christoph Volckamer published his two-volume *Nürnbergische Hesperides* (1708, 1714). This, too, contained excellent engravings of citrus

Besler: Hortus Eystettensis.

fruit, but included in the engravings illustration of individual gardens (pl. 33). Volckamer was a wealthy merchant and heir to his grandfather's silk factory in Rovereto, which enabled him to indulge in the expensive pastime of growing citrus fruits. A number of artists worked on this book, including Paul Decker the Elder, the Nuremburg-born engraver and architect. Tribute is paid to the influence of Ferrari by the inclusion of an engraving by Andrea Sacchi from Ferrari's *De Florum Cultura*.

A work that is not easily categorized is by the Dutch doctor and botanist Abraham Munting, who cultivated a variety of plants from all over the world. His *Naauwkeurige Beschriyving der Aardgewassen* (1696), published thirteen years after his death, contains decorative and rather strange engravings showing the plants, and below them, a variety of sometimes unrelated landscapes and scenes (pl. 34). The illustrations are by Jan Goeree and engraved by Jan Baptist.

The pleasure to be derived from flowers was felt strongly in Holland. And it is with this part of Europe in the late sixteenth and early seventeenth century that we particularly associate the still-life painting of flowers in their own right – not merely as symbolism or background decoration. Many of the artists who specialized in flower painting were also involved in the illustration of flower books.

It was in the Netherlands that the extraordinary 'tulipomania' began. The mania had its beginning in the love of flowers and in the interest in new varieties. Wilfred Blunt, in his book *Tulips and Tulipomania*, has described the strange episode and Abraham Munting in the book already mentioned devotes several pages to its history – an early account of the affair in which Munting's father himself had taken part. A hundred years later Johann Beckmann in his *History of Inventions* (1780) also gave an account of it. Describing how the plant originally came from Turkey, Beckmann writes:

> The Turks, who in other respects are not very susceptible of the inanimate beauties of nature, were the first people who cultivated a variety of them in their gardens for ornament and pleasure.

The first tulips in northern Europe were seen in Augsburg in 1559 and, according to Hakluyt, they were first planted in England at the end of the sixteenth century. Beckmann maintains that Hakluyt was 'wrong in ascribing to Clusius the honour of having first introduced them to Europe; for that naturalist only collected and described all the then known species.'

The extraordinary trade and speculation in tulips which lasted, at its height, from 1634 to 1637 had nothing to do with the love of flowers or gardens. At the same time it could not have been a trade or gamble in some manufactured article since much depended on the nature of the tulip itself. Tulips can be grown from seed. After about seven years these seedlings flower and are of one colour. They are breeder bulbs. These bulbs and their offsets may continue producing the same coloured flowers or they may, after an unknown time, suddenly 'break', producing a variegation. This was what the Dutch gambled on. Everyone grew tulips. At first they changed hands at enormous prices. Later all pretence at actually exchanging tulip bulbs was given up and the addict entered the realms of pure speculation. Rich and poor alike gambled with all they had. Fortunes were made and lost. Like most manias of this kind it suddenly collapsed. Beckmann wrote:

> The tulip trade may well serve to explain stock-jobbing of which so much is written in gazettes, and of which so many talk in company without understanding it. . . . It, however, cannot be denied that learned men may be infected with epidemical follies.

Morison: Plantarum Historiae.

One of the happier results of this particular 'epidemical folly' was the production of tulip books, mostly in manuscript. Essentially these were sale catalogues to enable bulb dealers to sell their wares. However, the tulip was such a phenomenon, in the seventeenth century particularly, that many florilegia have fine plates showing different species of the flower. We have already seen an example from Clusius, Dodoens and from de Passe (pls. 11, 12, 25 and 26). We have seen Besler's beautiful examples (pl. 30). Pierre Vallet, 'brodeur ordinaire' to Henri IV and to Louis XIII, included them in his *Jardin du Roy* (1623) (pls. 35, 36). The *Theatrum Florae* published anonymously by Daniel Rabel in 1622 shows tulips on its title-page and half-title as well as in full-page engravings (pl. 37). Toward the end of the century Robert Morison, in his history of plants in Oxford, *Plantarum Historiae Universalis Oxoniensis* (1680–99), also includes a page of tulips, the drawings for them having been made by Willem Sonmans, a Dutch artist working in England.

Perelle: Maisons Royales de France.

The gardens of Le Nôtre and their influence

In 1650 the powerful French financier Fouquet had commissioned the architect Le Vau to build a château (large country house or palace) at Melun, south of Paris. André Le Nôtre (1613–1700) was given the job of designing the gardens. Vaux-le-Vicomte was not designed for any innocent 'vie champestre', but was to be the theatre for tremendous display and for fêtes. The aim was to impress by grandeur and size, not by charm. If 'I am monarch of all I survey', was the principle, then the further you can see the better. We have come a long way from the enclosed garden of the Middle Ages.

After the downfall of Fouquet, Le Nôtre was employed by Louis XIV on the construction of the gardens at Versailles. Louis was anxious that Versailles should outdo Vaux-le-Vicomte in its grandeur and its ability to stun the beholder. Le Nôtre succeeded. He designed the gardens on a central axis straight through the centre of the house and, on the garden side, stretching as far as the eye could see (pl. 39). The eye was further disciplined by the trees (mainly hornbeams and beeches) planted on either side of the line of vision. The trees were kept clipped. At Versailles the main axis going from the palace into the distance consisted of a great *allée* of grass, at Vaux it was an expanse of parterres, but it could also be an area of water. Among the trees on either side of the *allée*, there were surprises consisting of open-air theatres, fountains, 'bosquets', all designed to create the variety which was thought desirable to soften the monotony of geometrical and symmetrical layout, and to provide novelty for members of the Court, who were only too easily bored. All the fanciful effects were carefully tucked away out of sight of the main vista. The woods were cut by avenues arranged in such a way that certain points formed the focus of minor radiating vistas: this *patte d'oie* or goose-foot effect was designed to make the spectator (or the King) feel that he was at the centre from which everything radiated. Statues were carefully placed against the dark trees, but flowers had little place in the scheme of things. At first Le Nôtre had left the parterres designed by Boyceau for the original château at Versailles, but later these were replaced by water and spectacular fountains (pls. 39, 40).

One of the main problems at Versailles was the lack of water. And since water was an essential part of the fashionable château, water had to be found. The problem was never satisfactorily solved. Attempts were made to bring water by canal, aqueduct and a number of reservoirs from the River Eure. Some 30,000 soldiers, including Swiss guards, were engaged in the task for several years. As the ground was swampy many caught a fever and many died. It became possible to have fountains, canals, water parterres and a water theatre, but water was always in short supply and the waterworks were only turned on when the King was in residence. The Duc de Saint-Simon was not filled with admiration for the King's achievements at Versailles (only the Trianon seems to have pleased him) and there is an echo of Francis Bacon in his comment on the waterworks:

Van der Groen:
Den Nederlandse Hovenier.

> La violence faite par-tout à la nature, dégoûte malgré soi; l'abondance des eaux forcées et ramassées de toute part, les rend vertes, épaisses, bourbeuses; elles répandent une humidité malsaine et sensible, une odeur qui l'est encore plus: leur effets qu'il faut pourtant beaucoup ménager sont incomparables; mais de ce tout, il résulta ce qu'on admire et qu'on fuit.

> [One cannot help but be revolted by the violence done to nature everywhere. The quantity of water collected from all sides and forced here makes it green, thick and muddy; it exudes an unhealthy and perceptible dampness and an odour that is even worse. It is true that the effects of the waters are incomparable . . . but the whole thing in the end inspires both admiration and repulsion.]

Saint-Simon found the ostentation of Versailles unspeakably vulgar.

Although many of Le Nôtre's basic concepts are to be found in most of the gardens designed by him, their ground plans are far from identical. Chantilly was one of the more unusual. Le Nôtre was commissioned by Prince Louis II de Condé, the 'Grand Condé', to design the grounds at about the same time as he began work at Versailles. The problems were different. Chantilly was a medieval château with Renaissance gardens. And there was plenty of water. Here, Le Nôtre found an almost Bramantean solution by devising a magnificent flight of steps from the terrace in front of the house down to that part of the garden which consisted of water parterres. There were shady avenues of trees and *allées* cut through the forest with *pattes d'oies* to provide vistas, and there were canals and magnificent waterworks. The château, however, does not lie on any axis of view, but rather in an angle of the grounds (pls. 41 and 42).

Other gardens designed, or partially remade, by Le Nôtre (such as Fontainebleau, Saint-Germain, Meudon, Saint-Cloud, the Tuileries or Sceaux) were all in the grand manner. Most of these gardens, where they survived at all, were changed out of all recognition by the French Revolution and then by the passion for the style of English landscape gardening which was to take Europe by storm.

One of the artists to whom we are indebted for records of gardens in France in the seventeenth century, and particularly for records of Versailles, is Gabriel Perelle, a contemporary of Le Nôtre. Perelle specialized in topographical paintings and engravings, particularly of Paris and Versailles, in his *Receuil des plus belles maisons royales de France*.

Le Nôtre himself never published any treatise on his principles of garden design, but much of it was done for him by Antoine Joseph Dezallier d'Argenville (1680–1765) who published the first edition of his *La Théorie et la pratique du jardinage* anonymously in 1709 – nine years after the death of Le Nôtre. In 1712 the book was published in English translated by John James (pls. 43, 44). Subsequent French editions were published in 1715 by LSAIDA (Le Sieur A J D'Argenville) and in 1722 by 'Le Sieur Alexandre Le Blond'.

Kleiner: Jardins de Plaisance

Le Nôtre's designs were all for gardens of great size. To have more popular appeal his principles would have to be adapted to smaller acreages. This d'Argenville did. The principles he formulated were that the house should be set at a higher level than the gardens, which in their turn should be so situated as to be neither so high as to be exposed nor so low as to be damp. Water was considered essential, a view an advantage and the site should, if possible, be convenient for practical purposes. The advantages of parterres, bosquets, *boulin-*

grins (though rarely used as bowling-greens in France), the covered walks, woods, hedges, canals, waterworks, labyrinths, statues, trellises; all are discussed for their individual merits and for their relationship to one another in the general layout. Parterres are discussed in some detail and the different kinds defined.

A book such as this helped to spread the fashion for the formal French symmetrical garden as Le Nôtre had perfected it. Large formal gardens appeared in a number of European countries. Sometimes the underlying principles were misunderstood or they were adapted to local conditions and taste. The Dutch enjoyed smaller formal gardens with flower beds or flower parterres, with designs rather less elegant than those in France. Dutch gardens were domestic rather than grand and had a tendency to be cluttered with topiary, statues and trellised walks.

Bonnefons: Le Jardinier François.

In England, despite the popularity of James's translation of d'Argenville, and despite the fact that most of Europe was hypnotized by Versailles, no such grand concept was made reality. There was no Louis XIV, and although many rich and powerful persons may have liked to show their wealth, they did so in a more modest manner. For one thing, most Englishmen wanted a garden that they would not merely look at, but could actually move about in. The view from the palace at Versailles stretching ahead as far as the eye can see is very impressive, but the idea of walking or even driving along the line of vision – which, in any event, was not intended – is essentially boring. English gardens remained more idiosyncratic. The gardens at Melbourne Hall in Derbyshire, for instance, still have many original French features adapted to the more modest English garden of the seventeenth century. They had been laid out by John Rose, a pupil of Le Nôtre. Rose in his turn had taught George London, who also worked at Melbourne. Between 1704 and 1711 the gardens were remodelled by Henry Wise, London's partner in the Brompton Nursery. Included in the garden was a waterpiece, a bosquet, alleys with statues or other ornaments at their intersections and the whole designed on a central axis. Nevertheless it was, and still is, an English and not a French garden.

At Hampton Court, Charles II changed the design of the grounds to one that was basically French: again John Rose was in charge. An engraving by Kip shows that much of the layout of Hampton Court was perhaps the nearest to a purely formal garden on the French pattern that was achieved in England. William and Mary, with George London as the royal gardener, soon added some Dutch touches by the building of smaller canals, and by statues and trees in pots. They also levelled the mound that had remained in the Tudor garden.

George London was part-owner of the Brompton Nurseries in Kensington and took on Henry Wise as a partner in 1694. The nurseries were large and successful and their owners were responsible for the work in many of the great gardens of England in the early part of the eighteenth century. They were the last to design gardens in the formal style. London and Wise translated Jean de la Quintinye's *Instruction pour les jardins fruitiers* into English and published it as *The Compleat Gard'ner*. John Evelyn had earlier also translated this work – with the same English title – by the gardener of Louis XIV. (De la Quintinye was the man responsible for the practical gardening, the growing of fruit and vegetables, whereas Le Nôtre was the landscape gardener.) London and Wise also translated Louis Liger's *Jardinier fleuriste* and Francois Gentil's *Jardinier solitaire*, which they published together as *The Retir'd Gard'ner* (pl. 45) in 1706. They added contributions of their own to all these works.

Munting: Naauwkeurige Beschriyving.

The botanist's century

Matthiolus: Opera quae extant omnia.

The humanist search for knowledge and understanding had affected the botanist and physician as much as any other group of men. Clusius's descriptive work on plants – many of which he had introduced to northern Europe – led the way for later botanists. The setting up of botanical gardens throughout Europe, starting with Padua and Pisa in 1545, was further evidence of the desire for a scientific approach to the subject.

Before 1735 the state of botanical classification was confused and inconsistent. Although botanists had frequently attempted to devise a variety of systems, none had proved satisfactory. Even relatively simple matters, such as ordering plants from nurserymen, caused difficulties. To try and remedy this, the Society of Gardeners published the *Catalogus Plantarum* (pl. 46) in 1730 to illustrate new plants. This work was largely in the hands of Philip Miller, the gardener of the Chelsea Physic Garden (of the Apothecaries' Society), whose important *Gardeners' Dictionary* was published a year later.

With no single consistent method of plant classification or nomenclature, a variety of flower books was published with decorative and often very accurate plates, though accuracy was sometimes sacrificed for the sake of decorative effect. There were works such as the *Exoticarum Plantarum* by the Danzig merchant and amateur botanist Jacobus Breynius (pls. 47, 48), which contains elegant and detailed engravings from drawings by Andreas Stech. Many of the 'exotic' plants in this book came from America. In Amsterdam, the Director of the Physic Garden was Jan Commelin, who was responsible for the *Horti Medici Amstelodamensis* (pls. 49 and 50). Commelin, who was an apothecary and dealer in simples (medicinal herbs), rather than a qualified physician, did much to further the scientific approach to the cultivation of 'exotics' in particular. The second volume of his book, which is devoted largely to plants from Africa, was written by Jan Commelin's nephew Caspar, who was professor of botany in Amsterdam. The engravings are made from water-colours by Johann and Maria Monickx and the publishers were P and J Blaeu, famous for their engraved maps.

A very remarkable figure from the late seventeenth and early eighteenth century was Maria Sybilla Merian. She was the daughter of Matthäus Merian the Elder, the engraver, and the grand-daughter of Johann Theodore de Bry, author of the *Florilegium Novum*. Early in her career she produced books on insects and flowers which she herself had illustrated. In 1698, at the age of 51, she set off for Surinam in South America with her daughter Dorothea. The result of two years' work on insects and flowers in Surinam was the *Metamorphosis Insectorum Surinamensium* published in 1705. Although Maria Merian was essentially an entomologist and the book is really devoted to insects, the execution of the botanical illustration is so fine that it is not unjust to rank her among the leading flower illustrators (pls. 56–8).

In 1735 Linnaeus published his *Systema Naturae* and so revolutionized the science of botany. His system is based on the famous binomial classification of plants (and animals) with two-word names, one for genus and one for species. After 1735 most flower books published earlier as florilegia based on no definite system of classification were botanically, though by no means aesthetically, out-of-date. The charming tributes that we find on the engraved title-pages of works such as those by Breynius or Besler to the 'fathers' of gardening (pls. 29, 48) vanish for ever.

Matthiolus: Opera quae extant omnia.

Inevitably many writers were at first reluctant to accept the new classification. Philip Miller's *Dictionary*, for instance, did not use the Linnaean nomenclature until the seventh edition in 1759, though his *Figures . . . of plants described in the Gardeners' Dictionary* (pls. 62–4) makes full acknowledgment and use of the new system. However, the *Figures* were not published until 1755–60, some twenty years after Linnaeus had first published his new classification. The delicate engravings include not only the whole flower but details of buds, stamens, sepals and other items necessary in a serious botanical illustration, without detracting from the aesthetic effect of the whole.

A work which was greatly influenced by Linnaeus, but which still belongs to the earlier period, was Robert Thornton's *Temple of Flora* (pls. 91, 92). Thornton had started his career as a doctor and had a successful practice. He was induced, through reading the works of Linnaeus, to abandon medicine for botany. In 1799, he started to publish the *Temple of Flora* (which formed part of his *New Illustration of the Sexual System of Linnaeus*). For the purpose he assembled the best painters, engravers and poets and exploited all the various processes of pictorial reproduction; the venture ruined him. Really the book is an old-fashioned florilegium, though the romantic backgrounds given to the plants sometimes come dangerously close to distracting the eye away from the plant entirely. There is no gainsaying the beauty of the plates though their accuracy is sometimes dubious.

Fülcken: Neue Garten Lust.

The work of Georg Dionysius Ehret, perhaps one of the greatest botanical artists, did much to introduce the Linnaean system. It was fortunate that the talent of Ehret and Linnaeus should develop simultaneously, their shared passion for knowledge, in particular botanical knowledge, finding artistic expression in the one – and scientific in the other. They met when Linnaeus was staying in Holland with his patron George Clifford to catalogue the plants in his garden. Ehret walked from Leiden to Haarlem to meet the naturalist. The result was their collaboration on the *Hortus Cliffortianus* (pl. 51), which was published in 1738 and which was the first book of botanical illustration based on Linnaean principles of classification and, therefore, the first scientific flower book. To accompany Linnaeus's description of the plants in Clifford's garden, Ehret drew twenty of the thirty-four illustrations. Nine of the others were drawn by Jan Wandelaar (1690–1759), who was also responsible for the engravings and the frontispiece. The plates are all uncoloured but are of great delicacy and accuracy and include details of different parts of the flowers.

Ehret's earlier patron and friend was the Nuremberg doctor Christoph Jakob Trew, who commissioned a number of botanical drawings from Ehret very early in his career. Ehret continued to send his drawings to Trew for many years from many different places where he happened to be working. They were published by Trew (and posthumously after his death in 1769) as *Plantae Selectae* (pls. 59–61) in serial form from 1750 to 1773. Trew was chiefly interested in drawings of exotic or unusual plants. Johann Jakob Haid, the Augsburg engraver, was engaged to make the engravings. His achievement seems some-

Fülcken: Neue Garten Lust.

what uneven; the Cereus (pl. 59) has caught the intentions of Ehret exactly, but the Lilium (pl. 61) seems rather harder and stiffer than the original drawing. (There are nearly a hundred drawings on vellum by Ehret in the Prints and Drawings Department of the Victoria and Albert Museum.) It is hard to assess Ehret's original work from engravings done by different hands, but there seems little doubt that Ehret was already at the height of his powers as a draughtsman and artist by the time the *Hortus Cliffortianus* was published.

After his work with Linnaeus in Holland, Ehret lived in England, where he made a great number of botanical drawings and had many rich patrons. His scientific accuracy together with the great beauty of his paintings combined to make him one of the greatest botanical artists of all time, and yet his popularity never equalled that of Pierre Joseph Redouté. Redouté was eleven when Ehret died in 1770 and two years later started to live as a travelling artist in the Netherlands. After a short career as a theatre artist with his brother, he was helped in his preferred career as a botanical artist by his first important patron, Charles Louis L'Heritier, for whose *Stirpes Novae* he made a large number of the original drawings. Also important in the development of Redouté's skill as a botanical artist was the painter Gerard van Spaendonck, who for a time was Professor of Natural History in Paris. He imparted to Redouté, as well as to many others, the particular skills of art and science that go to making the really great botanical artist. Redouté generally had his drawings engraved by stipple engraving and he used with it a method of printing from one plate in more than one colour – a method which he claimed to be of his own invention, though it is sometimes argued that it had been previously devised by van Spaendonck.

The Empress Josephine acquired the château of Malmaison in 1798 and was determined to cultivate a great variety of flowers there. She also wished to record these flowers. She therefore employed Étienne Pierre Ventenat as her botanist and Redouté as her artist. One of the results of their collaboration was the publication in 1803–4 of *Jardin de la Malmaison* (pls. 65–8). Redouté subsequently published a number of books that were instantly popular and remain so today. Notably his *Les Roses*, published in 1817–24, established him once and for all as the greatest of all botanical artists. His particular technique of colour printing contributed very greatly towards this reputation, but it is also undeniable that Redouté, in ignoring all trends of artistic fashion and in conveying directly his enthusiasm for the plant itself, put himself on to a different plane from all other botanical artists. Even Ehret does not always convey with such accuracy the delicacy and the fragility of a plant.

There were at the same time as Redouté a number of other excellent botanical artists working in Paris. The work of some was more aesthetically pleasing than botanically accurate or scientific. One of these was Jean Louis Prévost whose *Collection des Fleurs et des Fruits* (pl. 69) was published only two years after Redouté's *Jardin de la Malmaison*. It was intended more as a pattern book than as a serious botanical work. Although Prévost also used stipple engraving the result and the style are utterly different from the work of Redouté.

Morison: Plantarum Historiae.

Francis Andreas Bauer was exactly the same age as Redouté. He was one of the two German brothers who were both botanical artists. The younger, Ferdinand, was responsible for the illustrations in Sibthorp's famous *Florae Graeca*. Francis was persuaded by Sir Joseph Banks to join Kew Gardens as official botanical artist in 1790. In 1796 he made the drawings for the *Delineations of Exotick Plants Cultivated in the Royal Garden at Kew* (pls. 70–3). These 'exoticks' were South African ericas, or heaths, and they were drawn with the scientific accuracy as well as aesthetic understanding that, by now, we are beginning to expect from the foremost botanical artists of the eighteenth century. The engravings of Bauer's *Delineations* were made by Daniel Mackenzie, who had engraved the drawings made of plants during Captain Cook's voyage.

The process of aquatint was not used a great deal in botanical illustration though it was popular for topographical works. Flower illustration benefited more from the subtler and softer stipple engraving. However, at about the time when lithography (which Redouté turned to after 1835, but was not happy with) superseded line engraving in popularity, one beautiful flower book using aquatint was published. This was Mrs Edward Bury's *Selection of Hexandrian Plants* (pls. 74–8), which was published in 1831–4. The engravings were the work of Robert Havell, who also engraved Audubon's famous *Birds of America*. The engravings are partly printed in colour and partly hand-coloured. Mrs Bury's illustrations, though accurate, are not scientific and include no detail of plant or flower. They do, however, include the decorative effect of the butterfly – a device that even Ehret often used in drawings which were designed more to please than for scientific accuracy.

After the middle of the nineteenth century there was a very distinct deterioration in the quality of botanical illustration, which even the invention of lithography did little to improve. There was, however, one exception. This was Walter Hood Fitch, who began his working life as a designer in a Scottish calico firm. He became a protégé of W J Hooker while the latter was Professor of Botany at Glasgow University. In 1841 Hooker came south to take up his appointment as Director of Kew Gardens and Fitch came with him. Fitch worked for the *Botanical Magazine* and was responsible for the illustrations in numerous botanical works. He also adapted the drawings of Indian artists and lithographed them for the *Illustrations of Himalayan Plants* by J D Hooker, who was to follow his father as Director of Kew Gardens (pls. 79, 80). Fitch combined a great command of the lithographic technique with an equally great facility in botanical drawing.

The increased interest in gardening and in plants led to the sudden rash of botanical periodicals that appeared at the end of the eighteenth and early nineteenth century. They were only marginally scientific. In 1787 William Curtis founded the *Botanical Magazine* (pls. 81–4). This was the first and most successful of them all, and continues today under the aegis of the Bentham-Moxon Trust, Royal Botanic Gardens, Kew. In the earliest volumes the drawings and engravings of many of the plates were by James Sowerby, who signed most of the plates he was responsible for. The plates are hand-coloured and, although attractive, are clearly not as painstakingly produced as those by the great masters of the art. Less successful financially, but closer to Curtis's heart, was his *Flora Londinensis* (pl. 85), which he began to publish in 1777 and which described the flora of the London area. The artists responsible for this were William Kilburn and James Sowerby. The plates are more elegant as well as including botanical details. James Sowerby founded his own periodical, *English Botany* (pl. 86), which survived from 1790 to 1814, but was inevitably limited by its subject area. Sowerby himself worked on the illustrations and made James Edward Smith responsible for the text. Henry C Andrews in many ways imitated the *Botanical Magazine* with *The Botanist's Repository* (pl. 87), which he published monthly from 1797 to 1815 with only a brief interruption. Andrews also published books on heaths, geraniums and roses. Many of the descriptions in the *Repository* are by

John Kennedy, a nurseryman who became Andrews's father-in-law. Benjamin Maund's *Botanic Garden* (pl. 88) was more of a do-it-yourself periodical with Maund himself doing the writing, editing and printing. The illustrations are mostly by E D Smith, but also by a number of women artists, including Mrs Bury. The charm of the illustrations makes it a superior publication to that of *The Botanist's Repository* of Andrews but all these publications to some extent reflect the decline of botanical illustration that was taking place.

Linnaeus: Hortus Cliffortianus.

Landscape gardens

*Repton: Observations on
. . . landscape gardening.*

The general ferment and excitement in the world of scientific botany and of botanical illustration in the eighteenth century is extraordinary. At the same time, a revolution in garden fashion and design was taking place.

The concept in Europe of gardens purely for pleasure had originated in Sicily under Islamic influence. From the south the changing styles of gardening gradually crept northward as different countries took the lead as arbiters of garden fashion: Florence and Rome, then France, and in the eighteenth century it was the turn of England. The change was gradual, but when it came it was radical. When the style of painting or architecture changes, new works or buildings are created, but those of the former style generally survive. In gardens, new fashions mean the destruction of the old. Few gardens today can give us any indications of the formal designs of former times, except where they have been consciously reconstructed. The Queen's Garden at Kew is an interesting example of such a reconstruction – where the individual plants are given bibliographical references relating to their first mention in an English herbal. The gardens at Ham House and at Temple Newsam outside Leeds have been reconstructed according to the old designs. We are dependent for our knowledge on a few survivors and on engravings, paintings or verbal descriptions.

The reasons for the upsurge of English predominance in the style which came to be known as 'landscape gardening' are very varied. Some were practical and economic: the upkeep of formal gardens was a costly business few English landowners could afford. The weather in England meant that gardens, to be properly enjoyed, had to be walked about in. They could not be treated as another room, an extension to the house in which to sit and admire the endless vistas or to enjoy a play. The rain made possible the cultivation of fine lawns. And traditionally, the English were greater lovers of nature and were becoming increasingly aware of the beauty of their own landscape. Nor had they ever been able to fall entirely for the classical formality of Le Nôtre's style.

Much of the initial impetus for change was artistic and literary, rather than practical. The first critics of the old style were poets and essayists, and much of the inspiration for change came through art. The young gentlemen who went on the Grand Tour at this time came back fired with enthusiasm not only for Italian scenery but also for the paintings of Claude, Poussin and the wild landscape paintings of Salvator Rosa. This led to an enthusiasm for nature, not as we think of it today but in the rather idealized manner of these painters. This in turn led to a reaction against the geometric formality of the French garden and the subjugation of nature to art and artificiality that it required. There was, at the same time, a reaction against the domesticity of the Dutch style of gardening with its topiary, statuary and geometric flower beds.

Matthiolus: Opera quae extant omnia.

Writing in his periodical, *The Spectator*, in 1712, Joseph Addison attacked the 'mark of scissors' in gardens, the cutting of plants into unnatural and ridiculous shapes. He advocated the need for harmony between nature and art in the layout of a successful garden: 'I would rather look upon a tree in all its luxuriancy and diffusion of boughs and branches, than when it is thus cut and trimmed into a math-ematical figure: and cannot but fancy that an orchard in flower looks definitely more delightful than all the little labyrinths of the most finished parterre.'

Addison, Richard Steele, Alexander Pope, the very first arbiters of fashion in gardens at this time, were not architects or gardeners, but poets, essayists and literary critics. However, Pope did more than just criticize. He put his theories into practice in his garden of not much more than five acres at Twickenham. He managed in this small area to give an illusion of space by concealing the boundaries of the garden, by irregular planting and by winding paths. He added an obelisk, a grotto and other architectural features.

Sir John Vanbrugh, dramatist and architect, working at Castle Ho-ward, persuaded Henry Wise to leave a wood to grow naturally rather than cut it into a star shape. London and Wise designed a formal garden near the house itself, but further away from the mansion the classical buildings dotted about at specific vantage points in a more informal landscape heralded the first of the great landscape gardens.

Stephen Switzer was a practical gardener, a pupil of London and Wise, who worked in many of the great English gardens. In 1718 he published his *Ichnographia Rustica*. Despite his advocacy of increasing informality, he was moderate in his approach, and the illustrations in his book belie his text – they are still very formal. Switzer was influenced by the opinions of Addison and Pope, and so was Batty Langley, whose *New Principles of Gardening* was published in 1727. Langley favoured the judicious placing of ruins to end a vista (pl. 53). Ruins greatly appealed to the Romantics of the early nineteenth century, but they made their appearance in landscape gardens in the eighteenth century. A ruin of this kind can still be seen today in a number of gardens: the arch at Kew is an example.

It is not only in Switzer's work that we see the struggle between the formal and the 'natural' styles. The engravings by Rocque and Bedesdale in *Vitruvius Britannicus* (1739), show the two styles existing side by side. While James Worsley's Pilewell is formal, Henry Pelham's Surrey garden in Esher is 'modern' with woods growing naturally and with winding paths, though once again the formal design close to the house remains. These last gardens had been laid out by Pope's friend, the artist, architect and landscape designer William Kent. Horace Walpole's remark that Kent leapt the hedge 'and saw all nature was a garden' gives the impression of a sudden conversion. In fact, Kent was a forerunner of change and cautious: much of his work still clung to formality, though the influence of the painters began to be noticeable. In designing the garden of the villa of his patron, Lord Burlington, at Chiswick, Kent used a mixture of the old and the new styles. He then worked at Rousham in Oxfordshire, and here he created a garden which was conditioned by the lie of the land, though it still retained many artificial features. Kent then came to Stowe. The gardens here were designed successively by Charles Bridgeman, William Kent and then Capability Brown, and each left his mark, so that even today it is possible to see the changing ideas of garden design in the eighteenth century. Thomas Whately, a literary critic and politician, as well as a gentleman of taste and arbiter of fashion, praised Stowe in his *Observations on Modern Gardening* (1770), but felt doubtful about the quantity of buildings contained in the grounds as decorative features:

> . . . The multiplicity of the last [buildings] has indeed been often urged as an objection to Stowe; and certainly when all are seen by a stranger in two or three hours, twenty or thirty capital structures, mixed with others of inferior note, do seem too many; but the growth of the wood every day weakens the objection, by concealing them one from the other; each belongs to a distinct scene; and if they are considered separately at different times, and at leisure, it may be difficult to determine which to take away: yet still it must be acknowledged that their frequency destroys all ideas of silence and retirement: magnificence and splendour are the characteristics of Stowe.

Langley: New principles of Gardening

As time passed, the new ideas gained a stronger hold. Increasingly canals, straight avenues, formal parterres and topiary all vanished in favour of lawns and woods. Later, the one person most blamed for this obliteration of the old was Lancelot Brown. Capability Brown was the first practical gardener to have a truly revolutionary effect on the British gardening scene and can with justification be called the father of landscape gardening. Many of his gardens still exist today, fully matured or even past their prime, but certainly nearer what Brown envisaged than when they were first laid out. Whereas the formal garden was, in a sense, an 'instant' garden, the eighteenth-century landscape garden required imagination to foresee how it would look when the vegetation had matured and the trees grown to their full height.

Capability Brown's trade mark was the sweeping lawn, the clump of trees and the irregularly-shaped water surface. There was nothing here of the wild romanticism of a canvas by Salvator Rosa; everything was peaceful and the natural look was totally contrived – but subtly so and with an appearance of naturalness.

To achieve this Brown inevitably had to destroy most of the work of his predecessors, though not all. At Blenheim, for instance, it is the combination of Brown's work on the river and lake with Vanbrugh's bridge that is so particularly successful, though part of the success is

ngley: New principles of Gardening.

perhaps due to the restoration of some of the earlier formality at the beginning of the twentieth century.

Capability Brown's work was triumphant: from 1751 until his death he received innumerable commissions and, of course, had many imitators. Like Le Nôtre he never published anything on his theories of landscape gardening.

Brown's detractors, however, were not slow to put pen to paper. One of these was William Chambers, whose *Dissertation on Oriental Gardening* was published in 1722. Chambers had started work in the employment of the Swedish East India Company, in whose service he had three times been to the Far East, twice to China. Having decided that a mercantile career was not for him, he trained as an architect and became one of the foremost official architects of his time. In his *Dissertation* his attack on gardening fashion was two-pronged: against the old formal style and against the new. Of the old:

> The gardens of Italy, France, Germany, Spain, and of all the other countries where the antient style still prevails, are in general mere cities of verdure; the walks are like streets conducted in straight lines, regularly diverging from different large open spaces, resembling public squares; and the hedges with which they are bordered, are raised, in imitation of walls, adorned with pilasters, niches, windows and doors, or cut into colonades, arcades and porticos;. . . . not a twig is suffered to grow as nature directs; nor is a form admitted but what is scientific, and determinable by the line or compass.

Of the new:

> In England . . . our gardens differ very little from common fields, so closely is common nature copied in most of them; . . . and a stranger is often at a loss to know whether he be walking in a meadow, or in a pleasure ground. . . . At his first entrance, he is treated with the sight of a large green field, scattered over with a few straggling trees, and verged with a confused border of little shrubs and flowers; upon further inspection he finds a little serpentine path, twining in regular esses amongst the shrubs of the border, upon which he is to go round, to look on one side at what he has already seen, the large green field; and on the other side at the

boundary, which is never more than a few yards from him, and always obtruding upon his sight: from time to time he perceives a little seat or temple stuck up against the wall.

Chambers recommends the study of Chinese gardens. Chinese gardeners, he maintains, are highly trained:

They observe that mistakes committed in this Art, are too important to be tolerated, being much exposed to view, and in a great measure irreparable: as it often requires the space of a century, to redress the blunders of an hour.

This attack by Chambers may have been based on genuine dislike of Brown's work, or caused by pique at Brown's success (and Chambers's failure) to win a commission for the design of Lord Clive's garden at Claremont in Surrey. In any case, it was an important contributing factor to the predilection for chinoiserie, a preference to which Chambers himself gave expression with buildings such as the pagoda in Kew Gardens.

Chambers's attack on Brown and his work differed from the polemic that his successor Humphry Repton found himself engaged in. In 1788, five years after the death of Capability Brown, Repton, already thirty-six years old, decided to make landscape gardening his profession. To please his customers he devised what today would be considered a salesman's gimmick: his Red Books. These beautiful volumes, bound in red leather, were intended to show his clients by means of plans and watercolours how he would improve their estates. Using flaps (which he called 'slides'), he was able to show the design before and after his proposed changes. Similar illustrations in aquatint were subsequently used in his published books (pls. 89, 90). The use of 'slides' was not new. They had been employed as early as 1619 by Johann Remmelin in his medical book *Catoptrum Microcosmicum*, published in Augsburg by David Franck, to show the positions of human organs in relation to one another.

Repton: Observations on . . . landscape gardening.

In 1794, six years after he had begun work as a landscape gardener, Repton had already achieved great success. He had redesigned more than fifty estates and had published the first of his four books, the *Sketches and Hints on Landscape Gardening*. That same year saw the beginning of the controversy about the picturesque element in land-

*Repton: Observations on
. . . landscape gardening.*

scape gardening. Richard Payne Knight and Uvedale Price, both country landowners, believed that landscape painting – and particularly that of artists like Claude, Rosa and Poussin – should be the inspiration for landscape design, and they considered that Capability Brown's work in particular was far too unimaginative, suave and dull, and insufficiently picturesque. Repton, although acknowledging the importance of the picturesque in garden design, could not equate it with landscape painting. Gardening, in his view, had to take into account the practical needs of the inhabitants and was conditioned by the changing seasons and the shifts of light. Painting, on the other hand, idealized the natural scene and 'froze' it at a particular moment.

In his *Observations on the Theory and Practice of Landscape Gardening* (1803), Repton, writing about Bulstrode, said:

> This park must be acknowledged one of the most beautiful in England, yet I doubt whether Claude himself could find in its whole extent a single station from whence a picture could be formed. I mention this as a proof of the little affinity between pictures and scenes in nature.

And later in the same work he makes this statement of his ideas:

> I do not profess to follow either Le Nôtre or Brown, but selecting beauties from the style of each, to adopt so much of the grandeur of the former as may accord with a palace, and so much of the grace of the latter as may call forth the charms of the natural landscape. Each has its proper station: and good taste will make fashion subservient to good sense.

Thomas Whately had complained:

> It is a frequent error in our English gardens, that from the marble and gold and magnificence of a palace, we often step at once into all the wildness of the country.

This criticism did not apply to the later work of Repton. Unlike Brown, he came to believe in retaining some kind of formal design near the house: a parterre or a terrace to make the change less abrupt. The ha-ha kept the 'wildness of the country' close to the house without allowing the cows and sheep to peer in at the dining-room window. (Dezallier d'Argenville had mentioned the ha-ha in his book *La Théorie et la pratique du jardinage* in 1709. The English translation by John James of 1712 describes it as 'an opening which the French call a "Claire-voie", or an Ah, Ah with a dry ditch at the foot of it.')

At this time, the systematic search for new botanical specimens was being carried on overseas at an unprecedented rate and ever more new exotic plants were being introduced into English gardens. For a time flowers were still banished into a walled kitchen garden so that they would not spoil the idyllic setting of the landscaped garden or park. Repton's view in 1803 was:

> A flower garden should be an object detached and distinct from the general scenery of the place. . . . The flower garden, except where it is annexed to the house, should not be visible from the roads or general walks about the place. It may therefore be of a character totally different from the rest of the scenery, and its decorations should be as much those of art as of nature.

Flowers were allowed in the conservatory which was now becoming fashionable and necessary for the newer plants. Exotic shrubs and trees were later allowed by Repton to be planted near the house. There began to be signs that flowers, shrubs and colour were soon to flourish more openly than they had done for centuries: a foretaste of the 'Gardenesque' style to be promoted in the nineteenth century by John Claudius Loudon.

Loudon was essentially the landscape gardener of the middle classes, of the owners of suburban villas rather than of country estates. His idea.was that the gardener should so arrange his garden that the individual beauty of plants and trees might be displayed to best advantage (pls: 94, 95).

Colombina: II Bomprovifaccia.

The language of flowers

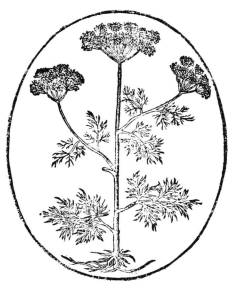

Thurneisser: Historia Plantarum.

The attitude of our ancestors to plants and flowers was at once practical and mystical. Practical, because every plant had its use either in the kitchen or in the sick room. Mystical, because of the belief in the power of plants to ward off evil, and the faith in their symbolism. Many botanists were alchemists or astrologers. Leonhardt Thurneisser, for instance, was definitely inclined to wizardry and to magic.

Today we have lost the magic and symbolism: we appreciate flowers for their beauty. When we use them in a ritualistic way, we hardly know the reason. When we use flowers at funerals, we are going back to a ritual of ancient Greece. The scattering of flowers on the dead symbolized the brevity of life, and, since the annual cycle brings renewal, it also symbolized death and resurrection.

The symbolism of flowers is a vast and complex subject and this is not the place to look at it in any detail. It is not possible here to do more than hint at some of its aspects, and to show the background of the sentimental Victorian 'language of flowers'.

The symbolism of gardens and flowers goes back to the beginning: to the idea of the Garden of Eden, to the concept of Paradise as a garden, probably through the ancient Persian word 'pairadaeza', which meant an enclosure of trees and fountains – a veritable paradise in a hot and dry climate. The Bible is full of floral imagery, richest in the *Song of Solomon*.

The meaning of the symbols varied according to the age and the place. In the Middle Ages in Europe, people were steeped in the symbolism of nature and every flower was full of meaning and hidden significance. The fifteenth century was one of the most magnificent for floral imagery. People at that time looking at a tapestry, a book of hours, a painting or the carved capital in a church rich in floral decoration, knew what message the artist was trying to convey. Although one symbol might have a number of meanings, some were accepted as being limited to certain interpretations. The lily signified purity, the lily-of-the-valley humility, the violet modesty. When our fifteenth-century ancestors looked at the picture of a vase containing roses, irises and lilies standing near the Virgin, they knew that they were looking at flowers symbolic of the virtues of Mary: her virginity or chastity, her majesty and her purity. Even the vase was symbolic. When they saw a painting of the Virgin in a rose garden they were confronting a mass of symbols. The rose had been used by the Romans as a symbol of victory, the joy of life or love triumphant and, perhaps most important of all, the flower of Venus. With the coming of Christianity the rose became the symbol of martyrdom. The early church had problems with the symbolism of the rose. It was difficult to transfer a symbol which had stood for the love of life and for passionate love to one representing death by martyrdom or for the Virgin Mary. However, gradually, the rose came to be accepted as the symbol for divine love and divine passion.

Colours of flowers were also significant. When a rose was white, it stood for purity, if red for martyrdom. Massed roses in garlands or baskets represented heavenly joy, and a single rose divine love. Although the rose is perhaps the flower to which the greatest amount of symbolism is attached, a comparable richness in imagery applies to the majority of other flowers.

In the sixteenth and seventeenth centuries another, stranger, form of allegory and symbolism was contained in emblem books. Woodcuts and engravings served as pictorial devices and these were accompanied by mottoes, epigrams, short sentences or poems by way of interpretation or elaboration. In emblem books, which could be profane or, more commonly, sacred, flowers and gardens were sometimes used to represent the various allegories. The Jesuit *Partheneia Sacra*, which is attributed to Henry Hawkins and appeared in about 1630, was at once an emblem book and a manual for devotion, a combination which was not uncommon. The enclosed garden is used as a symbol for the Virgin Mary and in the garden are placed flowers, trees and birds emblematic of her. In all there are twenty-four symbols or emblems associated with Mary, each representing one devotion.

The whole shows a mystical responsiveness to nature and to the medieval 'hortus conclusus' or enclosed garden.

By the eighteenth century most flower symbolism had lost its meaning, although some of the more obvious floral symbols were still recognized. The nineteenth century in England saw a rather confused revival – through the work of the Pre-Raphaelites – in mystical art and symbolism. At the same time, that sentimental and frivolous form of symbolism manifested in books devoted to the 'Language of Flowers' became popular. These were entertainment rather than folk mythology. It was a genre which, in its early years, often combined a surprisingly high standard of illustration with very sentimental and jingly rhymes. As it coincided with a time when flower painting was the accomplishment of practically every well-educated young lady, some quite remarkable illustrations can be found. The Victoria and Albert Museum Library is fortunate to possess several volumes of such a work in manuscript with flower paintings of a very high quality by a number of persons (pls. 102, 103). With a similar text, but with illustrations carried out by William Clark, at one time draughtsman to the London Horticultural Society, is Mrs Hey's *Moral of Flowers* (pls. 99–101), of which the Library also possesses the original paintings and manuscript. All these were produced in the 1830s – at about the same time as Robert Tyas's *The Sentiment of Flowers* (pl. 93) was published.

Despite the high quality of these illustrations, and the promise of lithography, the sad decline of botanical illustration continued, hastened perhaps by chromolithography and not changed for the better by photography. However, in recent years there has been a revival of interest in the herbal and in the art of illustration. These interests are not merely nostalgic, but are creative: and although new herbals must lack the spontaneity of the early specimens, there is no reason to abandon hope for the revival of the well-illustrated flower book.

Van der Groen: Den Nederlandse Hovenier.

Glossary

a

b

Alley or allée   In English gardens an alley was usually a walk or avenue flanked by hedges. In France, especially in the formal gardens and parks of Le Nôtre, an '*allée*' was a long avenue running between straight lines of controlled and clipped trees and woodland (fig. a).

Bosquet   A thicket of trees. In formal French gardens such thickets contained openings for open-air theatres or other areas to provide entertainments or agreeable surroundings for dalliance, such as the bosquet containing the 'Fontaine du Satyre' (fig. b).

Boulingrin   Literally a bowling green: an early example of 'franglais'. The *boulingrin* was a popular feature of the well-appointed garden in the late seventeenth century. John James gives a plan for the construction of a bowling green in his *Theory and Practice of Gardening* (fig. c).

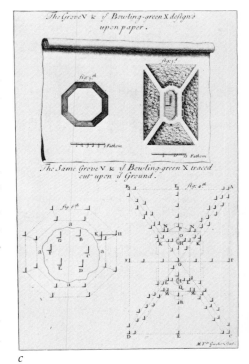

c

Grotto   An artificial cave, or room made to look like a cave, and often decorated with shells. Some grottoes had fountains or elaborate waterworks built into them. In architectural gardens with terraces and stairs, grottoes were often built under the terraces. Many grottoes built in the eighteenth century, when they were at the height of their popularity, still exist today (fig. d).

Herbal   A book containing the names, descriptions, virtues and properties of herbs and plants. Early herbals were usually compiled by physicians, herbalists or apothecaries.

d

Knots These were flower beds laid out in complicated geometric patterns. They became popular at the beginning of the sixteenth century. They were either planted on flat ground or on raised beds contained by boards or tiles. Van der Groen in his *Nederlandse Hovenier* (fig. e) shows a garden knot, and many early books on gardening contained a variety of patterns as suggestions for gardeners. The geometrical divisions usually consisted of low shrubs such as box, thrift or yew

e

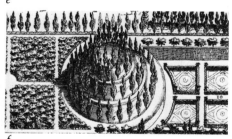

f

g

h

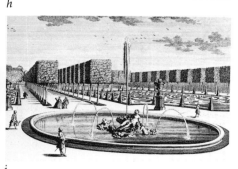

i

and they were filled with other shrubs or flowers, and later with coloured sands.

Mounts   These go back to the days of thirteenth-century monastery gardens, when earth was piled against the walls to provide a look-out into the outside world. By the late fifteenth century they had become very popular decorative features standing independently, away from the wall. We can see that even as late as the seventeenth century William Lawson puts a mount in each corner of his garden. From Tudor times on the mount was covered with turf and trees, with an arbour of some kind on the summit. The path leading to the top was usually a spiral with herbs or aromatic shrubs growing at the sides. The Villa Medici had a mount as in Falda's engraving (fig. f).

Parterres   These developed out of the knot beds. They are more complex, consisting of flowing arabesque designs. Where a bed is divided into sections by paths, the different sections did not necessarily contain symmetrical designs. Van der Groen's plan for a parterre in the French style (fig. g) shows how complex and convoluted the designs could be. They were also known as *parterres de broderie* and many designs show that the patterns could equally well be used for embroidery. Parterres could be of turf, of shrubs and flowers like a knot bed, or of water, such as those at Versailles and Chantilly.

Patte d'oie, or goose foot   A point in a garden where a number of straight paths or *allées* met, creating vistas in a number of different directions from a single point (fig. h).

Pleached alley   The word 'pleach' came from the Old French word *plessier* meaning to entwine or interlace. A pleached alley is a walk shaded by arched trees grown and cut in such a way as to intertwine overhead. The trees used for this were often hornbeams, white thorn, wych elm, willows or limes (fig. i).

An outline of the illustrative processes

Processes of illustration are generally divided into three kinds:

the first is the *relief* method where everything on the block or plate is cut away leaving only the surface to be inked and printed;

the second is the *intaglio* method whereby the line to be printed is cut in a groove on the block or plate. The ink fills the groove and is forced on to the paper when both the block and the paper are forced through a press;

for the third process the image is drawn (not cut) on to a surface: lithography is a method of this kind.

Woodcut.   This is a relief method. It had been in use in Europe since the late fourteenth and early fifteenth centuries, and sixteenth and early seventeenth century herbals and flowerbooks were illustrated by this process. The wood used was smooth grained, such as cherry, lime or maple, and was cut along the grain. It had the advantage that, being the same process as the printing of text, illustration and text could be printed in one operation. Technically the process of wood-cutting became increasingly perfected: one only needs to compare the illustrations in plate 1 and plate 5. However, printers realized that goldsmiths were already using a medium which was easier to handle than wood: engraving on a metal plate. In the seventeenth century printers turned increasingly to copper-plate engraving as an illustrative process, and by the eighteenth century it replaced the woodcut entirely. Woodcuts were revived in the eighteenth century by Thomas Bewick. They were in fact *wood engravings*, since he used a burin or graver on the end grain of a piece of wood – usually boxwood or yew. Many modern botanical illustrators use this process, which makes possible the creation of very subtle lines and tones.

Line engraving on metal.   As we have seen, this is a process adapted for book illustration from the art of the goldsmith. It is the intaglio method and consequently cannot be printed in the same operation as the printing of text, except in the case of some brief botanical information, such as the name of a plant, which can also be engraved on to the plate. In this process a smooth copper-plate is cut by the use of a graver or burin. This is a V-shaped cutting tool with a round

Van der Groen: Den Nederlandse Hovenier.

Bonnefons: Le Jardinier François.

wooden handle which fits into the palm of the hand and is pushed over the surface of the plate gouging out the metal in a V-shaped groove, which can be of whatever depth the engraver wishes. Printer's ink is forced into the grooves but wiped from the surface of the remainder of the plate. The plate, with dampened paper over it is then put through a roller press forcing the paper into the inked grooves. When the paper dries the inked lines stand out in relief. A comparison of even the best woodcuts such as that by Hans Weiditz (pl. 5) with that of de Passe or Johann Leypold (pl. 30) shows how much the scope of the engraver was enlarged by the use of copper-plate engraving.

Etching. This process also uses a metal plate, generally of copper. This is first covered with a protective ground and then smoked to make it dark. The artist then draws his picture on to this surface with a pointed needle so as to cut through the protective coating to the surface of the copper. The etcher holds the pointed tool like a pencil, and so has greater freedom of movement than the engraver. The plate is then put into an acid bath so that the lines which have been exposed by the needle are eaten into and deepened. If the artist wishes to deepen some lines more than others he can protect those that are deep enough by 'stopping them out' with protective material and exposing the others to more acid until the desired effect is achieved. Before the ink is applied all the protective ground is removed.

Line engraving remained the most popular illustrative process until the invention of lithography at the end of the eighteenth century. However, there were other variations of the intaglio method, and for the botanical artists the most popular of these were:

Mezzotint. For this process the metal plate is prepared by roughening it with small dots by means of a 'rocker' – a toothed tool that cuts into the metal by being rocked over it. When the entire plate has been covered in this way, the design is scraped on by smoothing the roughened parts. Lights and semi-tones can be obtained by the use of a burnisher for smoothing the plate, or of a scraper to remove some of the 'burr' thrown up by the rocker. The *Catalogus Plantarum* (pl. 46) published in 1730 and John Martyn's *Historia Plantarum Rariorum*, published 1728–36, used this method. Mezzotint was particularly popular for portraiture and Ehret's portrait (pl. 60) is engraved in mezzotint.

Stipple engraving. This technique used both etching and engraving.

It consisted of stippling dots on to a metal plate with a needle or a 'roulette'. This method was used particularly by Redouté, who devised a method of stipple engraving in several colours from one plate. It was also used by Jean Louis Prevost.

Aquatint. This process is an extension of the etching technique, adding washes to etched lines. By the use of different strengths of acids on a metal plate covered with a porous ground, great subtleties of tone and texture can be achieved. Mrs Bury's *Selection of Hexandrian Plants* (pl. 74) is illustrated by aquatint, which was introduced into England in the late eighteenth century, and first used to any significant extent by Paul Sandby.

Surface printing. The third illustrative process is *surface* printing, and the most important technique of this kind is *lithography*. A thick stone or zinc plate is used, and the illustration is drawn on its surface with a greasy crayon or ink. The drawing is fixed to prevent the greasy lines spreading and the stone is then wetted with water. When greasy printer's ink is applied it will be held by the greasy lines and repelled by the wet surface, so that only the greasy drawing is printed. Lithography was 'invented' or discovered by Alois Senefelder in Germany in about 1797. It flourished in England as a particularly delicate and successful illustrative process for the first half of the nineteenth century and was frequently used for botanical illustration. Walter Fitch (pl. 80) was a master of the art, which declined rapidly, particularly after the introduction of chromolithography in the 1830s.

Colour. The colouring of engravings was achieved by a variety of processes. At first all colouring was done by hand on to the finished engraving. In some cases we can see that the lines of the engraving were deliberately left thin to facilitate hand-colouring by the purchaser of the herbal. Sometimes the artist himself would apply the colour, sometimes others – frequently women or children – were employed to do so. Aquatint, mezzotinting and stipple engraving are processes in which colour could be applied to the plate and printed. In some instances different colours are applied to the plate in turn for each impression, in some several plates were used each with a different colour, and in a third all the necessary colours could be applied to the same plate and only one impression made. It was also possible to mix colour printing and hand-colouring. Chromolithography was not an aesthetic success when used in botanical illustration as its colouring was too coarse, and lacked the delicacy and refinement of earlier processes.

Matthiolus: Opera quae extant omnia.

Select bibliography

The first section of the bibliography lists the books that I have found most helpful as works of reference, both on botanical illustration and on garden history.

The second section lists the short titles of some of the herbals, flower books and books important in garden history that are in the Library of the Museum. They represent only a selection and are not necessarily first editions or the only editions in the Library. The dates given are those of the editions that I have chosen for the illustrations or for discussion in this book.

Matthiolus: Opera quae extant omnia

AMHERST, A M T   *A History of Gardening in England*. London: Quaritch, 1896.

ARBER, A   *Herbals, Their Origin and Evolution*. Cambridge: University Press, 1938.

BLUNT, W   *The Art of Botanical Illustration*. London: Collins, 1950.

COATS, A   *The Book of Flowers: Four Centuries of Flower Illustration*. London: Phaidon, 1973.

CRISP, F   *Mediaeval Gardens*. London: Bodley Head, 1924.

DUNTHORNE, G   *Flower and Fruit Prints of the 18th and Early 19th Century*. London: Dulau, 1938.

GOTHEIN, M L   *A History of Garden Art*. London: Dent, 1928.

GREEN, D   *Gardener to Queen Anne, Henry Wise (1653–1738) and the Formal Garden*. London: OUP, 1956.

HADFIELD, M   *Gardening in Britain*. London: Hutchinson, 1960.

HAZLEHURST, F H   *Jacques Boyceau and the Formal French Garden*. Athens, USA: University of Georgia Press, 1966.

HENREY, B   *British Botanical and Horticultural Literature before 1800*. London: OUP, 1975.

MASSON, G   *Italian Gardens*. London: Thames & Hudson, 1961.

NISSEN, C   *Die Botanische Buchillustration*. Stuttgart: Hiersemann, 1966.

PRAZ, M   *Studies in Seventeenth-Century Imagery*. Rome: Edizioni di Storia e Letteratura, 1964.

ROHDE, E S   *The Old English Herbals*. London: Longman, 1922.

STROUD D   *Humphry Repton*. London: Country Life, 1962.

STROUD D   *Capability Brown*. London: Faber, 1975.

AGRICOLA, G A   *The Experimental Husbandman and Gardener*. London: Mears, 1726.

ANDREWS, H C   *The Botanist's Repository*. London: Bensley, 1797.

ANDROUET DU CERCEAU, J   *Les plus excellents bastiments de France*. Paris, 1607.

BAUER, F   *Delineations of Exotick Plants*. London: Aiton, 1796–1803.

BESLER, B   *Hortus Eystettensis*. Eichstätt & Nürnberg, 1613.

BOYCEAU, J   *Traité du jardinage selon les raisons de la nature et de l'art*. Paris: Van Lochom, 1638.

BREYNIUS, J   *Plantarum Exoticarum Centuria Prima*. Danzig: Rhetius, 1678.

BRUNFELS, O   *Herbarum Vivae Eicones*. Strassburg: Schott, 1530–32.

BRY, J T de   *Florilegium Novum*. Oppenheim, 1612.

BURY, Mrs E   *A Selection of Hexandrian Plants*. London: Havell, 1831–34.

CALMANN, G   *Ehret, Flower Painter Extraordinary*. Oxford: Phaidon, 1977.

CAUSE, H   *De Koninglycke Hovenier*. Amsterdam: Doornick, 1676.

CHAMBERS, W   *Dissertation on Oriental Gardening*. London: Griffin, 1772.

CLUSIUS, C   *Rariorum Aliquot Stirpium*. Antwerp: C. Plantin, 1576.

COLOMBINA, G   *Il Bomprovifaccia*. Padua: Tozzi, 1621.

COMMELIN, J   *Horti Medici Amstelodamensis*. Amsterdam: Blaeu, 1697.

CURTIS, W   *Flora Londinensis*. London, 1777–98.

CURTIS, W   *The Botanical Magazine*. London, 1787–(still current)

DE LA QUINTINYE, J   *Instruction pour les jardins fruitiers*. Paris: Nyon, 1716.

DEZALLIER D'ARGENVILLE, A J   *La Théorie et la pratique du jardinage*. Paris: Mariette, 1709. (This edition published anonymously.)

DODOENS, R   *Stirpium Historiae Pemptades Sex*. Antwerp: C. Plantin, 1583.

EVELYN, J   *The Compleat Gard'ner*. London: Gillyflower, 1693.

FALDA, G B   *Li Giardini di Roma*. Rome: Rossi (1670?).

FERRARI, G B   *Hesperides sive De Malorum Aureorum Cultura*. Rome: Mascardi, 1646.

FERRARI, G B   *Flora, seu De Florum Cultura*. Amsterdam: Jansson, 1664.

FUCHS, L   *De Historia Stirpium*. Basel: Isingrin, 1542.

FÜLCKEN, J D   *Neue Garten Lust*. Augsburg: Pfeffel (1750?).

GARDINER, J   *Rapin: of Gardens, a Latin Poem . . . English'd by Mr Gardiner*. London: Lintot, 1728.

Gerard: The Herball

Matthiolus: Opera quae extant omnia.

GERARD, J   *The Herball, or General History of Plantes.* London: Norton, 1597.

GRETE HERBAL   Southwark: Treveris, 1526.

GROEN, J van der   *Den Nederlandsen Hovenier.* Amsterdam: Doornick, 1669.

HEY, R   *The Moral of Flowers.* MS. 1831.

HEY, R   *The Moral of Flowers.* London: Longman, 1833.

HOOKER, J D   *Illustrations of Himalayan Plants.* London: Lovell Reeve, 1855.

HYLL, T   *The Profitable Arte of Gardening, Now the Thirde Time Sett Forth.* London: Waldegrave, 1586.

JAMES, J   *Theory and Practice of Gardening.* London: James, 1712.

KNIGHT, R P   *An Analytical Inquiry into the Principles of Taste.* London: Payne, 1805.

LANGLEY, B   *New Principles of Gardening.* London: Bettesworth & Batley, 1728.

LAUREMBERG, P   *Apparatus Plantarius.* Frankfurt: Merian, 1632.

LAWSON, W   *A New Orchard and Garden.* London: Sawbridge, 1676.

LIGER, L   *Le Jardinier fleuriste.* Paris: Savoye, 1764.

LINNAEUS, C   *Hortus Cliffortianus.* Amsterdam, 1737.

LODDIGES, C   *The Botanical Cabinet.* London, 1817–33.

LONDON, G & WISE, H   *The Retir'd Gard'ner.* London: Tonson, 1706.

LONDON: SOCIETY OF GARDENERS   *Catalogus Plantarum.* London, 1730.

LONICER, J A   *Kreuterbuch.* Frankfurt: Egenolffs Erben, 1569.

LOUDON, Mrs J   *Ladies Flower Garden of Ornamental Annuals.* London: Smith, 1840.

MATTHIOLUS, P A   *Opera quae extant omnia, hoc est commentarii in sex libros Pedacii Dioscoridis.* Frankfurt: N. Bassaeus, 1598.

MAUND, B   *The Botanic Garden.* London: Baldwin & Cradock, 1825–51.

MERIAN, M S   *Over de Voortteeling en Wonderbaerlyke Veranderingen der Surinaemsche Insecten.* Amsterdam: Bernard, 1730.

MILLER, P   *Figures of the Most Beautiful, Useful and Uncommon Plants, Described in the Gardeners' Dictionary.* London: Rivington, 1809.

MORISON, R   *Plantarum Historiae Universalis Oxoniensis.* Oxford, 1680.

MUNTING, A   *Naauwkeurige Beschryving der Aardgewassen.* Leiden & Utrecht: Van der Aa & Halma, 1696.

N, RDCDWBD (Nicolas de Bonnefons) *Le Jardinier françois* Amsterdam: Blaeu, 1654.

L'OBEL, M de *Icones Stirpium seu Plantarum tam Exoticarum.*
Antwerp: Moretus, 1591.

ORTUS SANITATIS Strassburg: Prüss, c.1500.

PARKINSON, J *Paradisi in Sole.* London: Thrale, 1656.

PASSE, C de *Hortus Floridus.* (French text.) Arnhem: Jansson, 1614–15.

PERELLE, G *Receuil des plus belles maisons de France.* Paris: Mariette (1680?).

PRÉVOST, J L *Collection des fleurs et des fruits.* Paris: Vilquin, 1805.

PRICE, U *A Letter to H. Repton Esq.* London: Robson, 1795.

RABEL, D *Theatrum Florae.* Paris: Mariette (1680?). (Published anonymously.)

REPTON, H *Observations on the Theory and Practice of Landscape Gardening.* London: Taylor, 1803.

ROBERTS, H MS of flower paintings. 1830–55.

SOWERBY, J *English Botany.* London: Davis, 1790–1806.

SWITZER, S *Ichnographia Rustica: or, The Nobleman, Gentleman and Gardener's Recreation.* London: Fox, 1742.

THORNTON, R *The Temple of Flora.* London: 1799–1807.

THURNEISSER, L *Historia sive Descriptio Plantarum Omnium.* Berlin: Hentzschke, 1578.

TREW, C J *Plantae Selectae.* Augsburg, 1750–73.

TYAS, R *The Sentiment of Flowers.* London: Tilt, 1837.

VALLET, P *Le Jardin du roy tres chrestien Loys XIII.* Paris, 1623.

VENTENAT, E P *Jardin de la Malmaison.* Paris: Crapelet, 1803–5.

VERGNAUD, J *L'Art de creer les jardins.* Paris, 1839.

VOLCKAMER, J C *Nürnbergische Hesperides.* Nürnberg: Endters' seel. Sohn u. Erben, 1708.

WHATELY, T *Observations on Modern Gardening.* 1770.

WOOLRIDGE, J *Systema Horti-culturae: or The Art of Gardening.* London: Dring, 1688.

Lauremberg: Apparatus Plantarius

The Plates

Fuchs: De Historia Stirpium

tae nata eft remonere:nö folum in arteria fed in fcabiofa vefica propter mediocritate comple rionis. ¶ Theodorus prifcianus. Ualet:ptra omia vitia pectoris decoctio eo? in aqua.et in pleureti. z peripleumonia. aqua decoctiöie ei? valet ptra tuffim. ¶ Ad idem valet electuarium facrum ex fucco liquiricie z melle. Liquiricia mafticata z fub lingua retenta fitim z afperitatem ftomachi z guttur mitigat.

¶ Dyafcorides. Uirtus eft micturalis. Radix eius alba eft fimilis panaci eracleontico z odorata. Uirtus eft radici z femini ei? calida z ftiptica doloribus oibus intraneo? occurrit. Inflāmationé ftomachi foluit. ¶ Cibo venenatis opitulat. vrinā prouocat. menftruis imperatis bibat. antidotis colicis profunt aut mifcet. ¶ Radix eius tunfa z fuppofita idem preftat.ra dix eius z femé ori porxis necefle mifcet pfectiö: nibetiam digeftibilibus vtiliter adbibet: qz eu ftomaca eft. vnde multi aucefipfius prouinne eo pro pipere vtuntur condituris mifcentes. ¶ Et multi femé fifelei z feniculi addunt illi. q̄ dam dicit q̄ eft leuifticū fed falfo.

Capitulum. cclx.

Igulfici. fm Dy af. cap. Liguftici mal ti nafcit in liguria prouincia. vnde z nomé accepit. nafcit z in montevicino alpibus: fed cius panacem illum vocant. ideo qz radix eius alba eft. z odorata fimul panaci. cui virtue vna eft cum panacis virtute. Nafcit in locis altis z afperis: z vmbrofis. virgam habet longam z nodofam fimilem anero. In qua virga folia funt fimilia melliloro. Sed molliora z odorata que folia in cucumere tenuiffima funt z diuifa. In virge fumitate caput z vmbraculofum. Ubi femé oftendit q̄ femen nigrū eft z oblongum ficut feniculi guftu vifcidū z odoratum aromaticum.

Operationes.

Inaria. pandecta.ca.Dic. Linaria é herba fimilis efiule vel lino: ppter q̄ vocatur. z differt ab efula q̄m eiula lactefcit linaria vero nö. vnde verfus. Efiula lacteícit fine lacte linaria crefcat. ¶ Operationes. ¶ Succus eius valet ʒ beris fiftulas inunctus. z cū fucco pinpinelle mixtus. ¶ Et ipfa fola valet ad cancrū irita et impofita. ad boc fimiliter fuccus eius valet.

Capitulum. cclx.

Imon. Pan. cap. ccccviij. Limon fructus pulchri odozoris. plen? fucco acetofo valde apro falfamétis. Et ipfe etiā comeditur fale conditus nufq̄ memini me de ipfo legiffe apud autozem autentici. nifi apud Auicennā in quarto canone de cura febrium acutarū in generali vbi iubet dari aquam acetofitatis limonis fallin.

Capitulum. cclxj.

Capitulum. cclxij.

Inu. vfi. Linū ex terre nitéti fpé ozif. nomé fumpfit a greco. vel q̄ leue fit ac molle. Biffum āt eft. gen̄ quoddā lini nimiū candidi ac molliffimi: q̄ grece paparen vocat. ¶ Pall. In fe. mefe aliū femé lini leto foflofpar gūt. z lina pfequunt exilia. ¶ Ité lib. ij. In mefe octobxi femé lini feri pxti placuerit. q̄ ti. p fui malicia ferendū nö eft: qz terre vber exhaurit. fz fi rebus loco pur giffimo. z modico hu mido ferere poteris. aliū macro folo fpiffum ferentes: fi affequunt vt linū fubtile nafcat.

Operationes.

¶ Sera li. ag. au. Fal. Uirt? eius é q̄ fubtiliat z. puocat vrinā z menftrua. z q̄n bibit aur fit cū ea emplin. pfert apatibus epatis. z orificio ftomachi z ipfi ftomacho. Sz radicie er? ftipricitas é ampliee ftipricitate floris. z calidiras er? eft minor caliditate ipfius. z. ppter er? ftipticitate acq̄ rit q̄ admifcet cū medicinis q̄ admiftrant ad fputi fanguis. ¶ Sera. au. Dyaf. Flos er? eft ftipricus ftipricitate panca calefacriuus. matu ratiuus. z eft ca. q̄ fin. i. g. é medtiī in bu. z fic. Et rad. eius fius é q̄ eft mollificatiuū. ¶ Sera li. ag. ca. barancdicbene. i. linū eft mollificariuū fedatiuū dolor. z pfert egritudinibus interiorbus nifi q̄ eft min̄ in fi q̄ camomilla. z é mediū inter laxatiuū z ftipticū. z admifcet in eo pax ʒ q̄ rutie. puocat me vrine. z b q̄é apparet i eo mani fefte q̄n comedit a flatu. z hic eft magie. puenit ad ftringédū ventré. ¶ Et dixit il. de pferuatoe fanitatis. q̄ q̄n femé lini decoquit in aq̄. eius de coctio é infrigidatiua. ¶ Et ideau. Dyaf. Uir tus feminis lini efilis fruti femis fenu greci. et q̄n admifcet cū aq̄ melle z oleo z oficit: z refoluit a pata ca. z mollificat ea. fiue funt interi? fiue exterius. z q̄n fit ex eo emplin cū ficibus nitro de let pannū z puftulas albas faciei. i. papulas fm tranfla. no. ¶ Dyaf. Et q̄n oficit cū aq̄ refoluit apata q̄ funt i radice aurie. z apata dura. Et q̄n coquit cū vino eradicat formica z fpés vlcer q̄ dicunt faui. z q̄n mifcet cū melle z pipere z vnt q̄s eo mouet coitū. z q̄n mifcet cū nafturtio. ipfi tate eq̄li pfert ficiffuris vnguiū z eo? excoriatoi. ¶ Et fir cū decoctöe er? crifter ad mordicatione inteftino? z matricis. z mollit ventré q̄n mulie res fedét in decocöe eius. pfert apatibus in atr cis fic fenugreci. ¶ Paulus ca. de lino. Linū q̄n cöburit. Fum? eius é fubtilis. z pfert cozize z fuffocarioi matricis. ¶ Auic.li.ij.ca. de feiel/ ni. Uirt? ei. prima fruti fenugreci. i. ca. cö mefurarū in humiditate z ficcirate. Et ez q̄ é q̄ decoctio lini eft decocrior cécétis eius. ¶ In ipa

q iij

1, 4 Ortus Sanitatis
Strasburg: Prüss, c. 1500
The woodcuts in this herbal are printed from the same block as the text. They were partly new and partly taken from the earlier German Herbarius or Gart der Gesuntheit of 1485. Some of the illustrations are realistic and others are fantastic. The mandrake root was for centuries surrounded by myths and superstitions, the chief one being that it had a human form and screamed when pulled from the soil.

2 Il Bomprovifaccia
Gasparo Colombina
Padua: Tozzi, 1621
A comparison of the illustrations in this book with those in the Ortus Sanitatis *(pls. 1, 4) shows how earlier woodcuts continued to be used with only slight modifications to illustrate herbals of a much later date, and how the illustrations were frequently not even intended to be realistic or to represent the plant concerned. The block for the 'ligu[s]ticum' in the* Ortus Sanitatis *has been changed only a little to illustrate the 'iride' in the Italian work.*

Iride.

H Anno l'Iridi tutte calda, e fecca natura per la qual caufa (dico Plateario) che fi può vfare

N   nelle

haue e bertue of tryacle but it wpl laſt but two yetes.

¶ For the breth B
¶ Agaynſt payne and lettynge of brethe cauſed of colde / Boyle dꝛye fygges / and capꝛyne in ſtronge wyne / and ſtreyne the and in ſtreynynge put therto halfe an vnce of powdꝛe of dꝛyptan / and gyue it to dꝛynke.

¶ For to delyuer a deed chylde. C
¶ To delyuet a deed chylde out of the moders wombe / and the webbe that it is in the woman. Make an intercꝑo oꝛ peſſaꝛye of the iuce of this herbe and medle y̆ powdꝛe of the rote therwith.

¶ For the fallynge euyll. D
¶ Agaynſt the fallynge euyll. Take the powdꝛe of dꝛyptan and of caſtoꝛeum conſeet with iuce of rue and ſtreyne it / & put of the ſame lyrout in to the pacyentes noſe and anoynte hym therwith warmed.

¶ De detonici. Ca. C.rlvi.

O Etonici ben lytel rotes of an herbe ſo named / and ben hote and dꝛye in the thyꝛde degre. Theſe rotes ben whyte g

ſmall full of knottes as the rotes of poliꝑ podion. Thep be good agaynſt paynes cauſed of wyndes and chefely of the matryce e bytynge of venymous beſtes. Therfoꝛe they be medled with theſe medꝑyns / and grete confectios oꝛdeyned agaynſt venim and in the lyke wyſe is galyngale.

¶ De Dactilis. Dates. Ca. C.rlvii.

'O ctilis be dates / thep be hote and moyſt in the ſeconde degre. Thep engendꝛe groſſe oꝛ couꝛs blode / & be harde of dygeſtyon / but thep be better of digeſty on than dꝛye fygges / and pꝛouoketh better bꝛyne. But who ſo vſed the moche falꝑ leth in opplacyon of the mylt and lyuer wᵗ hardneſſe and ſwellynge. Thep be noyons to the gommes and teth / and be of dluers acryons after dyuerſyte of regyons where thep gꝛowe. Foꝛ ſome gꝛowe in hote regyꝑ ons / ſome in colde / & ſome in meane. Thep that gꝛowe in hote regyons ben ſwete and glepmy / & gꝛueth but lytell nouryſſhynge and be ſoone dꝛgeſted & looſeth y̆ wombe.

But thep that gꝛowe in colde regyons abyde in theyꝛ raukeneſſe / and raweneſſe / bycauſe thep be leſſe nouryſſhynge of all y̆ other / and ben harde to dꝛgeſt. Howe be it thep confoꝛth the ſtomake moꝛe than ony of the other. Thep that gꝛowe in meane regyons ben not ſo hote / but thep map be kept longe yf thep be not gadꝛed oꝛ thep be rype. Thep haue ſuperfue lyroute by the whiche thep fyll the body and cauſe groſſe humours to habounde whiche often be cauſe of longe agues and acceſſe bycauſe thep be yll to ſpꝛed and deuyde.

¶ Thus endeth the chapꝑtres begynnynge with. D.
¶ And begynneth y̆ chapꝑtres begynnynge with .E.

¶ De endiuia. Endyue. Ca. C.rlviii.

A diuia is endyꝑ ue. It is colde & dꝛye in the fyꝛſte degre. It is other wyſe called ſcaryꝑ ole. The ledes & y̆ leues ben good in medꝑeyns / and the rotes haue no bertue / the gꝛene leues haue bertue & not the dꝛye. The leues haue a lytell bytterꝑ neſſe bycauſe thep be dꝛyretykes / and haꝑ ue pontycyte oꝛ raukeneſſe wherby thep be confoꝛtatyues / and by theyꝛ coldnes thep haue bertue to withdꝛawe and to coole / & al theſe thinges conioynte togider be good agaynſt opplacyon of the lyuer and of the mylte cauſed of heete.

¶ For the Iaundis D
¶ Agaynſt all maner of Iaundꝛs & chauſ fynge of the lyuer & hote apoſtumes. The leues eate rawe oꝛ ſoden in water helpeth moche / & foꝛ the ſame y̆ iuce medled with trifera ſaraſenica is good / but it behoueth y̆ the mater of y̆ ſekeneſſe be fyꝛſt dygeſted.

¶ For vnſauery mouthes. B
¶ For them that ſauour not theyꝛ meates make ſyrope of the iuce of endyue with ſuꝑ gre / & yf the iuce be thycke oꝛ troubled claꝑ ryfye it / & ſo mo al other iuces be / in this wyſe. Sethe the iuce of endyue a lytel and lete it ſtade / & that y̆ is thycke wyll go to the botom / than take the thynne lyrout & ſtreyne it often thꝛough a clothe but wꝛyn ge it not & with y̆ iuce clere as water maꝑ ke ſyrope with ſugre / yf ye wyll make it thynnet put y̆ whyte oꝛ glereꝑ of an egge therto. This ſyrope is good agaynſt the iauꝺꝛs. yf ye wyll make a laratyue ſyꝛoꝑ pe whan it is almoſt ſode put therto powꝑ dꝛe of reubarbe wel bete & ſtreyne it yf ye wyll not haue it byte / but yf it be ſtreined it is not of ſo good bertue as it is vnſtreined

---

3

3   The Grete Herbal
Southwark: Peter Treveris, 1526
Many of the woodcuts come from the German Herbarius (1485), the Ortus Sanitatis and other works. It was the first illustrated herbal in English. The illustrations are still printed from the same block as the text and, as in many early printed works, the whole is made to look like a manuscript, including the decorated initial.

Tractatus ... De Herbis

4

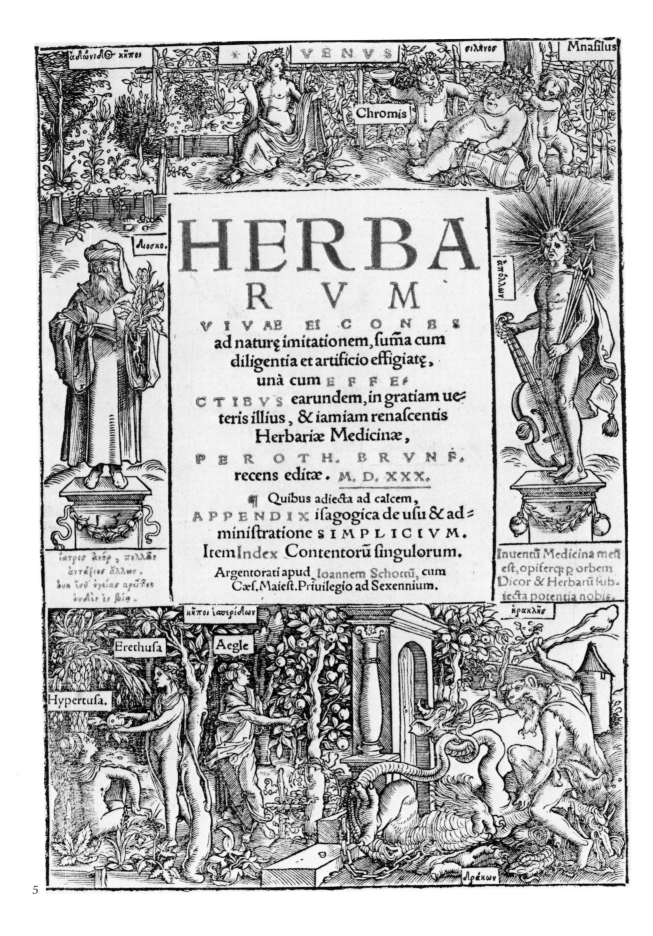

HERBA
RVM
VIVAE EICONES
ad naturę imitationem, suma cum
diligentia et artificio effigiatę,
unà cum EFFE=
CTIBVS earundem, in gratiam ue=
teris illius, & iamiam renascentis
Herbariæ Medicinæ,

PER OTH. BRVNF.
recens editæ. M. D. XXX.

¶ Quibus adiecta ad calcem,
APPENDIX isagogica de usu & ad=
ministratione SIMPLICIVM.
Item Index Contentorū singulorum.

Argentorati apud Ioannem Schottū, cum
Cæs. Maiest. Priuilegio ad Sexennium.

5, 6 Herbarum Vivae Eicones
Otto Brunfels (1488–1534)
Strasburg: Schott, 1530–36
The importance of this work lies in the
illustrations rather than in the text. The
draughtsman and engraver was Hans
Weiditz, a pupil of Dürer. Weiditz drew
from nature, presenting plants as they were,
even when they were damaged or fading.
The engraved title-page shows mythical
figures in sixteenth-century gardens. The
pasque flower is one of the most successful
engravings in this herbal: it combines
accuracy with aesthetic appeal and a feeling
for the form and texture of the plant. The
improvement in technique over previous
illustrations is very marked.

7, 8 De Historia Stirpium
Leonhard Fuchs (1501–66)
Basel: Isingrin, 1542
Once again the illustrations are more
important than the text. The lines of the
woodcuts seem rather thin, but they were
probably intended to be coloured by the
owner of the book. Unlike Weiditz, Fuchs
insisted that only perfect plant specimens
should be used for the illustrations.
The author fully acknowledged the work
done by the illustrators of his herbal by
including portraits of all three of them.
Heinrich Füllmaurer was the artist, Albert
Meyer transferred the drawing to the
woodblock and Veit Rudolf Speckle was
responsible for the engraving.

6

7

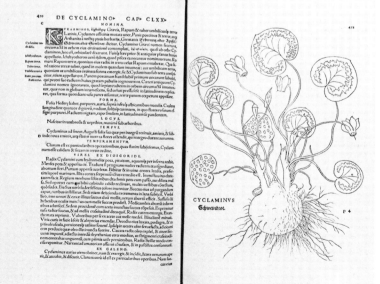

8

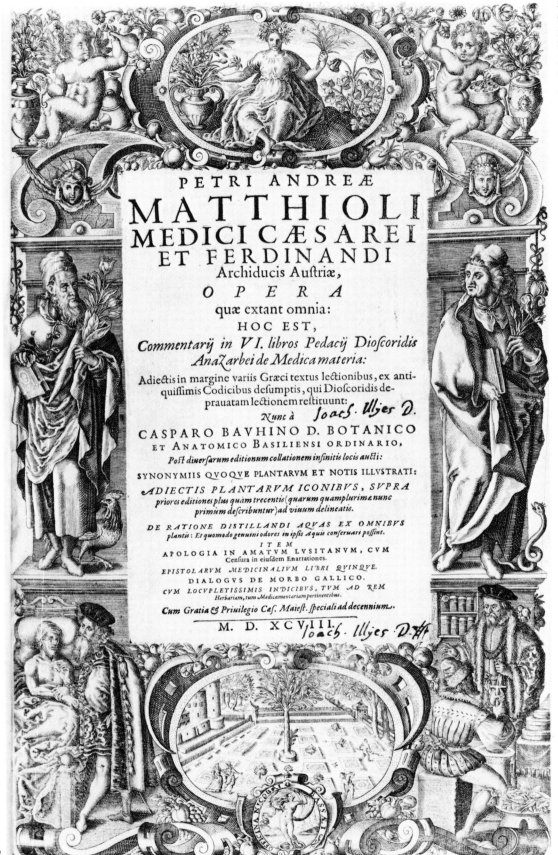

PETRI ANDREÆ
MATTHIOLI
MEDICI CÆSAREI
ET FERDINANDI
Archiducis Austriæ,
OPERA
quæ extant omnia:
HOC EST,
Commentarij in VI. libros Pedacij Dioscoridis
AnaZarbei de Medica materia:
Adiectis in margine variis Græci textus lectionibus, ex anti-
quissimis Codicibus desumptis, qui Dioscoridis de-
prauatam lectionem restituunt:
Nunc à Joach. Uljes D.
CASPARO BAVHINO D. BOTANICO
ET ANATOMICO BASILIENSI ORDINARIO,
Post diuersarum editionum collationem infinitis locis aucti:
SYNONYMIIS QVOQVE PLANTARVM ET NOTIS ILLVSTRATI:
ADIECTIS PLANTARVM ICONIBVS, SVPRA
priores editiones plus quàm trecentis (quarum quamplurima nunc
primùm describuntur) ad viuum delineatis.
DE RATIONE DISTILLANDI AQVAS EX OMNIBVS
plantis: Et quomodo genuini odores in ipsis Aquis conseruari possint.
ITEM
APOLOGIA IN AMATVM LVSITANVM, CVM
Censura in eiusdem Enarrationes.
EPISTOLARVM MEDICINALIVM LIBRI QVINQVE.
DIALOGVS DE MORBO GALLICO.
CVM LOCVPLETISSIMIS INDICIBVS, TVM AD REM
Herbariam, tum Medicamentariam pertinentibus.
Cum Gratia & Priuilegio Cæs. Maiest. speciali ad decennium.
M. D. XCVIII. Joach. Illjes D.

9, 10   Opera Quae Extant
Omnia, hoc est Commentarii
in VI libros Pedacii
Dioscorides etc
*Pietro Andrea Matthiolus
(1500–77)
Frankfurt: N. Bassaeus, 1598*

9

Matthiolus's commentary on Dioscorides appeared first in 1544 without illustrations. The edition shown here was edited and enlarged by the botanist Caspar Bauhin. It included many new engravings as well as some used by Joachim Camerarius in his German edition of Matthiolus published in 1586. The engraved title-page of the 1598 German edition was designed by Jost Amman, but the artist of the title-page of this Latin edition is uncertain.

11   Rariorum Aliquot Stirpium
Carolus Clusius (1526–1609)
Antwerp: C Plantin, 1576
This book, the first by Clusius, resulted from an expedition to Spain and Portugal during which he discovered many new species of plants. It can be seen from the illustrations here that the same block was used by Plantin for two different authors, and in fact the same block was also used in Icones Stirpium *by Matthias de L'Obel in 1581.*

12   Stirpium Historiae Pemptades Sex
Rembert Dodoens (1516–85)
Antwerp: C Plantin 1583
Many of the woodcuts in this work are original, but some, as can be seen here were used for the works by Clusius.

cenſuit Dod.hiſt.Gallica.At quam Matth.hoc loco expreſſit, non videtur aliud eſſe quàm Melanthium ſylueſtris nomine ſuperius propoſitum:ab eo tantùm foliis inferioribus Aniſum referentibus,differens Hunc imitari ſunt, Caſtor, Durantes, herbarij Lugdunenſis author,& Tabernæmontanus.

Ἴον πορφυροῦν.   VIOLA PVRPVREA.   CAP. CXVII.

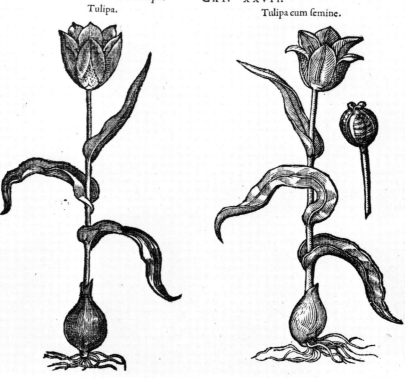

Viola purpurea folium habet hedera minus, tenuius,ac nigrius, nec multò diſsimile:cauliculus à radice medius prodit, in quo floſculus ſuauiſsimè olens, purpureus:opacis, & aſperis naſcitur. Refrigerandi naturam habet. Folia per ſe, & ex polenta illinuntur aptiſsimè ſtomacho æſtuanti, & oculorum inflammationibus,ſedique procidenti.

Sunt in Violarum genere non modò purpurea, ſed etiam candida, frigida & vliginoſis locis naſcentes, prorſus tamen inodora, de quibus nihil,quod extet, memoria prodidit ratio. Dioſcorides. Hæ numeroſa proueniunt in Ananienſi agro ſupra Tridentum, vbi menſe Aprili adeò copioſè florent, vt ſi longè proſpiciantur, oculos fallant,& extenſa lintea videantur. Sunt & alia, quæ aureo ſunt colore, adeò in colorandis floribus occupatur natura. Eſt & genus,Oeniponti primùm mihi viſum,cuius purpurei flores numeroſis ſtipantur foliolis, odore omnium iucundiſsimo. ARBORESCENTEM autem VIOLAM è Baldo monte in agro Veronenſi allatam, odore perquàm iucundo, mihi dono miſit Franciſcus Calzolarius pharmacopæus Veronenſis, cuius flores illis perſimiles ferè habentur, qui in Regali conſolida viſuntur. Creſcit hæc duorum cubitorum altitudine, pluribus ab vna radice ſublatis caulibus, in quibus folia violæ purpureæ anguſtiora, per ambitum denticulata, atque paribus interuallis diſtincta:flores edit purpureos.Aly præterea flores per æſtatem Maio,& Iunio menſibus viſuntur tribus reſerti coloribus,ſupernè purpurei, in medio candidi, inferius verò lutei, forma purpureas violas referentes, aſpectu gratiſsimo, cùm tamen nullo & ipſi commendentur odore. Prodeunt hi ex

Violæ purpureæ conſideratio.
Viol. purpur. multipl.
Viol. purpur. multipl.
Violæ arboreſcentis mentio.

quadam planta, cui primo exortu folia inſunt rotunda, per ambitum ſerrata, quæ tamen per incrementum in longitudinem deſciſcunt. Conſtat hac caulibus triangularibus,quadantenus ſtriatis,& intus concauis,quibus paribus inter‐

10

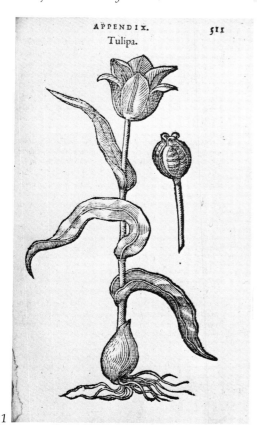

Tulipa.

1

De Tulipa.   CAP. XXVII.
Tulipa.   Tulipa cum ſemine.

12

THE
HERBALL
OR GENERALL
Historie of
Plantes.

Gathered by John Gerarde
of London Master in
CHIRVRGERIE.

Imprinted at London by
Iohn Norton.
1597

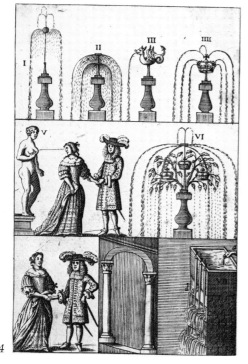

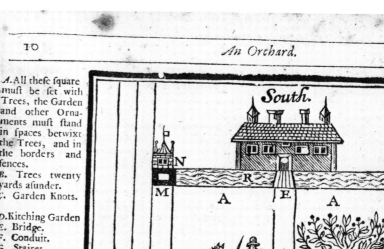

A. All these square must be set with Trees, the Garden and other Ornaments must stand in spaces betwixt the Trees, and in the borders and fences.

B. Trees twenty yards asunder.

C. Garden Knots.

D. Kitching Garden

E. Bridge.

F. Conduit.

G. Staires.

H. Walks set with great wood thick.

I. Walks set with great wood round about your Orchard.

K. The Out fence,

L. The Out fence set with stone-fruit

M. Mount. To force Earth for a Mount or such like, set it round with quick, and lay boughes of Trees strangely intermingled, the tops inward, with the Earth in the middle.

N. Still house.

O. Good standing for Bees, if you have an house.

P. If the River run by your door, and under your Mount, it will be pleasant.

4

15

13   The Herball

John Gerard (1545–1612)

London: Norton, 1597

Gerard was in charge of the gardens of Lord Burghley in the Strand and at Theobalds in Hertfordshire, as well as having his own garden in fashionable Holborn. Few of the woodcuts in his Herball are original. After Gerard's death a greatly improved edition was brought out by Thomas Johnson in 1633. The title-page was designed and engraved by William Rogers, one of the earliest English exponents of copper-plate engraving. It is interesting that the cartouche at the bottom of the title-page is very similar to that on Matthiolus's title-page. This may be explained by the fact that Norton, Gerard's publisher, obtained woodblocks from Frankfurt, where Matthiolus's herbal was published.

14   Systema Horti-culturae: or, The Art of Gardening

John Worlidge (Woolridge)

3 ed. London: Dring, 1688

Both this work (the first edition of which appeared in 1677), and the one by William Lawson were an indication of the popularity of this type of publication among the yeomanry.

As a result of Italian influence, fountains became an essential feature of the well-appointed garden in the Tudor period and remained so, becoming increasingly elaborate and designed to give the unsuspecting observer a sudden wetting.

15   A New Orchard and Garden

William Lawson

6th ed. London: Sawbridge, 1676

The first edition of this work appeared in 1618 and proved an instant success. The book also contains sections on 'The Country-House-wifes garden for herbs of common use' and 'The Husbandry of Bees, with their several uses and annoyances'.

16

16 Li Giardini di Roma
Giovanni Batista Falda (c. 1640–c. 1678)
Rome: Rossi, c. 1670
Falda did much to record the topography and
monuments of Rome in the seventeenth
century in his engravings.

17 Here the Vatican is shown after Pope
Sixtus V had built a library (4) across the
second terrace designed by Bramante,
thereby destroying one of the magnificent
staircases that had been so important in the
linking of the Belvedere and the Vatican,
and which had done so much to set the style
for the Roman Renaissance gardens.

18 The Quirinale, the Pope's palace at
Monte Cavallo, also as described by John
Evelyn, the fountain of porphyry is No. 15
and the hydraulic organ at No. 10 in the
engraving by Falda.

19 The Villa Medici, shown by Falda
much as John Evelyn described it: the loggia
(4) and arcade (3) with statues.

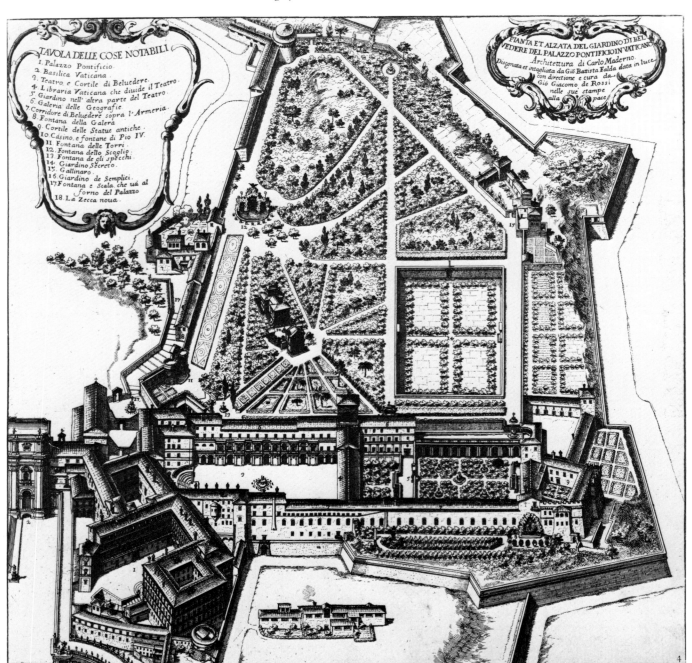

17

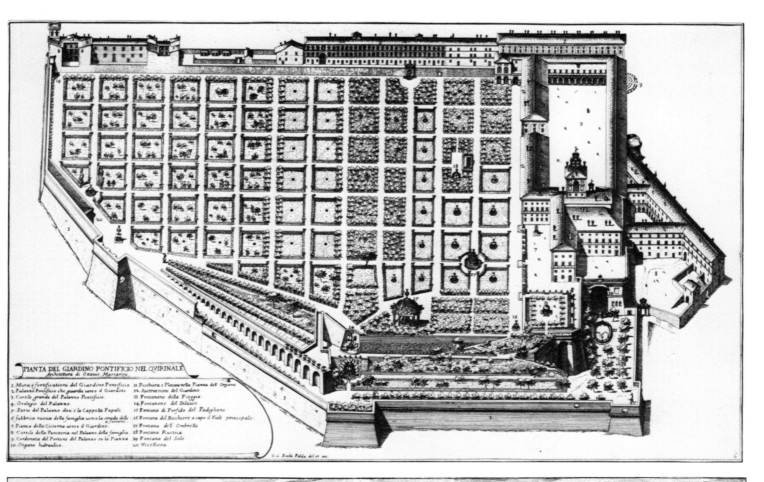

PIANTA DEL GIARDINO PONTIFICIO NEL QVIRINALE
Architettura di Onorio Maccarini

1. Mura e fortificationi del Giardino Pontificio.
2. Palazzo Pontificio che guarda verso il Giardino.
3. Cortile grande del Palazzo Pontificio.
4. Orologio del Palazzo.
5. Porte del Palazzo dou e la Cappella Papale.
6. fabbrica nuova della famiglia verso la strada delle fontane.
7. Piazza della Cisterna verso il Giardino.
8. Cortile della Panetteria nel Palazzo della famiglia.
9. Cordonata del Portone del Palazzo su la Piazza.
10. Organo hidraulico.
11. Peschiera e Platano nella Piazza del Organo.
12. Fontanone della Piazza.
13. Fontanone della Pioggia.
14. Fontanone del Diluuio.
15. Fontana di Porfido del Padiglione.
16. Fontana del Bucchero a capo il Viale principale.
17. Fontana dell'Ombrella.
18. Fontana Rustica.
19. Fontana del Sole.
20. Vccelliera.

Gio. Batta Falda del et inc.

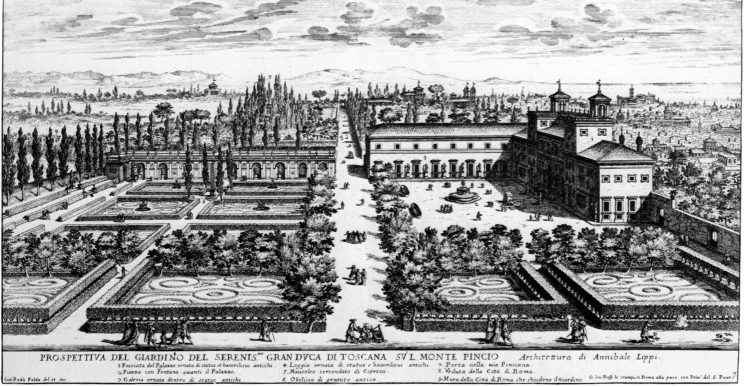

PROSPETTIVA DEL GIARDINO DEL SERENIS.mo GRAN DVCA DI TOSCANA SVL MONTE PINCIO   Architettura di Annibale Lippi.

1. Facciata del Palazzo ornata di statue et bassirilieui antichi.
2. Piazza con Fontana auanti il Palazzo.
3. Galeria ornata dentro di statue antiche.
4. Loggia ornata di statue e bassirilieui antichi.
5. Mausoleo cercondato di Cipressi.
6. Obelisco di granito antico.
7. Porta nella uia Pinciana.
8. Veduta della Città di Roma.
9. Mura della Città di Roma che chiudono il Giardino.

Gio. Batta Falda del et inc.   G. Iac. Rossi le stampa in Roma alla pace con Priu: del S. Pont.

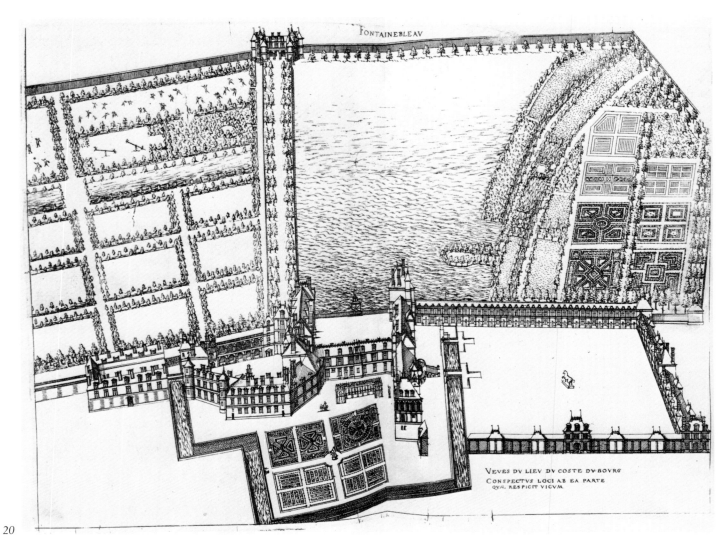

FONTAINEBLEAV

VEVES DV LIEV DV COSTE DV BOVRG
CONSPECTVS LOCI AB EA PARTE
QVÆ RESPICIT VICVM.

20

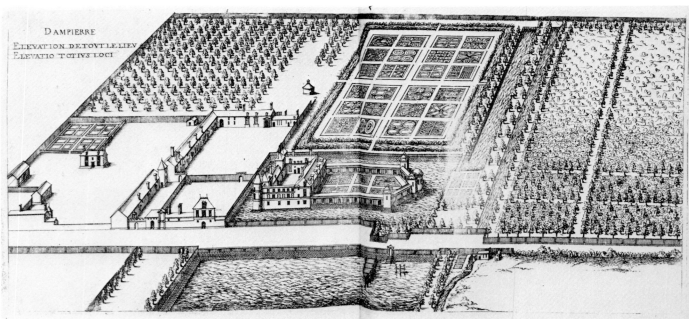

DAMPIERRE
ELEVATION DE TOVT LE LIEV
ELEVATIO TOTIVS LOCI

21

Les plus excellents bastiments de France
Jacques Androuet du Cerceau (c. 1510–
c. 1584)
2 ed. Paris, 1607.
Du Cerceau was the first of an eminent
family of French architects, known today
more for their activities as artists, engravers,
etchers and architectural theorists. The first
edition of this book – his best known –
appeared in 1576–9, and was dedicated to
Catherine de Medici. The engravings are by
Du Cerceau himself or were done under his
supervision.

20 Fontainebleau *Originally a hunting*
lodge, the château was built by Francis I
using Italian artists. In the gardens there
were canals, and a swamp was turned into a
lake, thereby setting a fashion for later
French Renaissance gardens.

21, 22 Dampierre *Androuet du Cerceau*
shows Dampierre as a typical early French
Renaissance garden with canals abounding.
One parterre, enclosed by turreted galleries,
is immediately in front of the château and
both are surrounded by walls and a canal.
There is another larger garden divided into
parterres by walks, also surrounded by
canals. There is as yet no sign of the house
being built on a main axis.

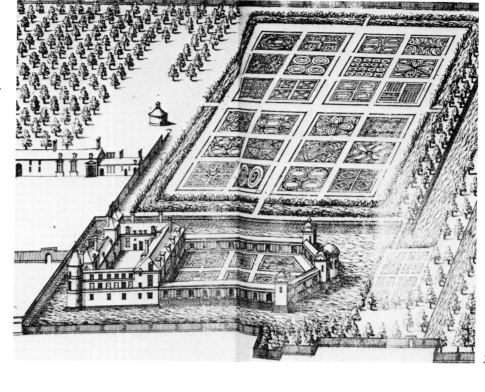

22

23 Traité du jardinage
Jacques Boyceau
Paris: Vanlochom, 1638
A hunting lodge was built for Louis XIII at
Versailles. This plate shows Boyceau's
design for the central parterre. It is similar
to the great parterre he designed for the
gardens of the Palais de Luxembourg.
Despite a superficial appearance of
symmetry, the pattern in each section is
different.

23

24 Paradisi in Sole Paradisus Terrestris *John Parkinson (1567–1650) 2 impr. London: Thrale, 1656 Unlike some earlier works, Parkinson's book – with the exception of its delightful title-page – is notable more for its text than its illustrations. The title-page was engraved by Christopher Switzer, whose name is visible in the bottom right-hand corner.*

25

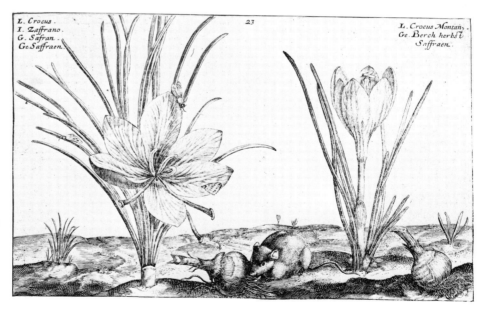

26

25, 26 Hortus Floridus
Crispin de Passe (1589–1670)
French version. Arnhem: Janssoon, 1614
This was one of the earliest florilegia and one
of the first botanical books with copper-plate
engravings. Crispin de Passe was the
principal contributor, though he was clearly
helped by his brothers Simon and Willem,
whose names appear on some of the plates.

Florilegium Novum,
Hoc est:
VARIORUM MAXIMEQUE RARIO-
rum Florum ac Plantarum singularium unàcum
suis radicibus & cepis, Eicones diligenter ære sculptæ
& ad vivum ut plurimum expressæ.

New Blumbuch
Darinnen allerhand schöne Blumen und frembde
Gewächs/ mit jhren Wurtzeln und Zwibeln/
mehrer theils dem Leben nach in Kupffer
fleissig gestochen/ zu sehen seind.
Exhibitum nuper, auctum.

A Iohanne Theodoro de Bry Ciue Oppenheimense. Aᵒ M.D.CXII

27

27, 28 Florilegium Novum
Johann Theodor de Bry (1561–1623)
Oppenheim, 1612–13
This was another of the earliest florilegia to
be illustrated by copper-plate engraving. The
work was popular and was published in a
number of editions. In 1641 an edition was
published by the engraver Matthäus
Merian, who had married de Bry's daughter
and who was the father of Maria Sybille
Merian. The architectural title-page
combines elegance and charm and lacks the
ponderousness of many later ones.

29, 30 Hortus Eystettensis
Basilius Besler (1561–1629)
Eichstätt and Nuremberg, 1613
This monumental work contains some of the
most decorative copper-plate engravings of
the period. Each of the four parts is devoted
to a season. The title-page is by Wolfgang
Kilian of Augsburg. Solomon and Cyrus
appear on a number of engraved title-pages
to flower books in the pre-Linnaean era. Both
were held to have been great gardeners,
Solomon presumably on the evidence of
Ecclesiastes and the Song of Solomon. Cyrus
was believed to have built a great garden at
Celenae.

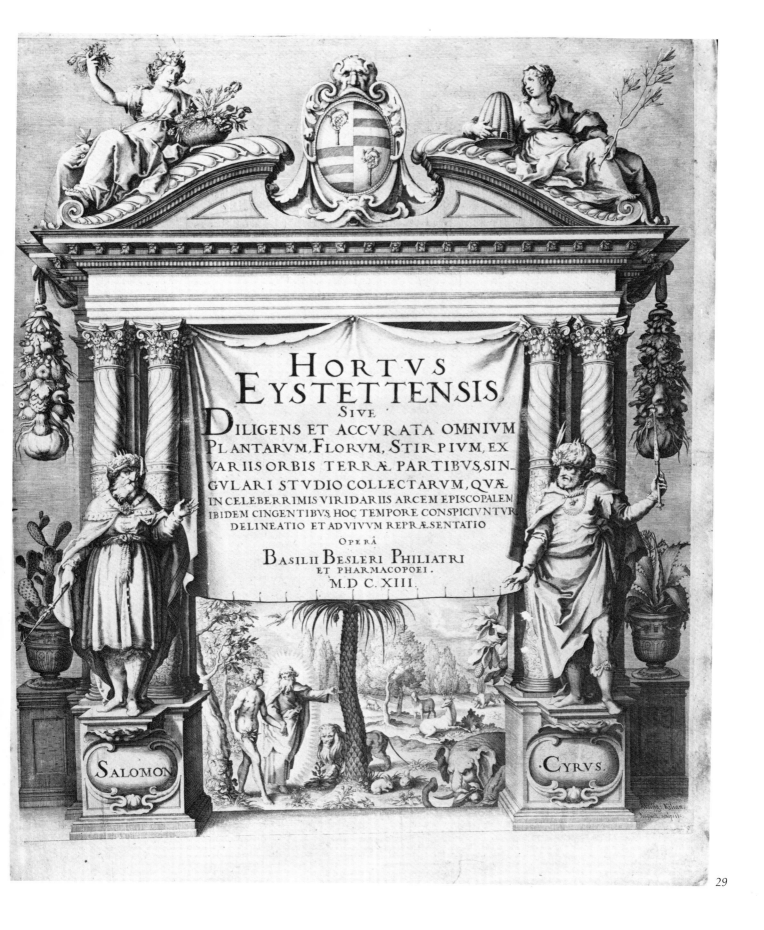

HORTVS EYSTETTENSIS,

SIVE

DILIGENS ET ACCVRATA OMNIVM
PLANTARVM, FLORVM, STIRPIVM, EX
VARIIS ORBIS TERRÆ PARTIBVS, SIN-
GVLARI STVDIO COLLECTARVM, QVÆ
IN CELEBERRIMIS VIRIDARIIS ARCEM EPISCOPALEM
IBIDEM CINGENTIBVS, HOC TEMPORE CONSPICIVNTVR
DELINEATIO ET AD VIVVM REPRÆSENTATIO

OPERÂ

BASILII BESLERI PHILIATRI
ET PHARMACOPOEI.

M.DC.XIII.

SALOMON

·CYRVS·

Tulipa purpurea calice
pallescente.

Tulipamuei coloris,o,
ris rubeo purpurascen,

IV.

Tulipa ex pallido tota vi,
rescens.

V.

Tulipa flav. sulphur, co,
lore pallescentibus lituris pro,
pe apices roseis flammiformib,

III.

II.

Tulipa floribus flexis inferi,
miniatis, exterius herbaceis
margine ex cinnabari ru,

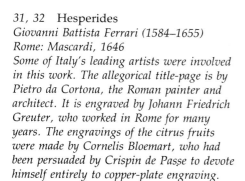

Limon pyri effigie, vulgò Peretta, sive Spataforà.
Cap. XI.

VT in limone pyri faciem præuideremus auribus, saporemque iisdem prælibaremus : decuit hunc vulgu Perettam nominari. Vt idem pomaria illuſtrior habitaret : à nobiliſſimo, qui ſuos tranſtulit in hortos, Siculo viro Spataforæ cognomen accepit. Porrò autem geminus eſt, nempe minor & maior, ſi Peretta : verus & falſus, ſi de aliorum ſententia Spataforà dicatur. Priori turbinatio pyri cuiuſdam ſerotini, quod recentiores Bronchium ſiue Florentinum appellant. Cortex oppidò granoſus, languidè luteus, & iucundè olens, mediumque floris prætenuem apicem exertus : caro minimùm digitalis : medulla modica, ſeptenis octoniſue ſpicis diſtincta, citraque auſteritatem ſuauiter acida : pauca ſemina : magnitudo varia : rhegino ſumma in ſolo librarum ferè quatuor. Arbos ramuloſa, nonnullis aculeis hiſpida, & iniurijs cæleſtibus opportuna. Rami perquàm fragiles, in latera proni, & frequentium onere pomorum ſæpius nutantes laborantesque, ægrè in cælum tendentes. Folium longulum, denſiſſimum & ſatis virens. Flos citrino porrectior, dubio foris rubore ſuffuſus, ramorum ſæpe lateri adnaſcens, interque foliorum denſitatem ſemiconſpicuus. Totum eſtur pomum, pyri ſapore palato gratiſſimum, ſtomacho tamen incommodum : quia cortice duriuſculum ægrè vincitur. Limon alter non abſimilis prædicti minoris pomi præſtantiam ſapore non æquat : etiamſi longiore ornetur folio, duploque vel triplo maior, vt corpore, ſic nomine augeatur, dum grandior Peretta dicitur. Eius arbor rhegino in agro, vt ipſi aſſerunt populares, mira magnitudine adoleſcit : totoque anno vberrimè ſpecioſéque parit. Aliam alibi raram inuentu Perettam neapolitanus ager, agreſtium quoque ſertilis miraculorum, Romam nuper tranſmiſit ad Ioannem Baptiſtam Martellettum : ne lectiſſimis floribus conſimilia poma in hoc amœnitatum campo cultorem optimum inuiderent. Quare limon hic meritò ab eo, qui Romanum fecit, Martelletti nomen accepit. Eius breuitas vulgari Perettæ compar, forma diſpar, imis anguſtis in pediculi commiſſuram exertis, ventre in rotunditatem compacto, apice in mucronem turbinato, ſtrijs ab imo pomo ad ſummum ſic procurrentibus, vt in medio ſeſe laxantes vtrinque coëant. Cortex coloris modice fluſi, & odoris iucundi. Caro craſſitudinis exiguæ. Medulla palloris ſulphurei, nouem circiter ſpicarum, acoris arguti, nulliusque ſeminis. Hic

Limon pyri effigie triplici nomine. Minor.

Maior.

Striatus.

Ioſ Baptiſtæ Martellettus

31

Giovanni Battista Ferrari (1584–1655)
Rome: Mascardi, 1646
Some of Italy's leading artists were involved
in this work. The allegorical title-page is by
Pietro da Cortona, the Roman painter and
architect. It is engraved by Johann Friedrich
Greuter, who worked in Rome for many
years. The engravings of the citrus fruits
were made by Cornelis Bloemart, who had
been persuaded by Crispin de Passe to devote
himself entirely to copper-plate engraving.

32

Lima dolce. 1699

In Hrn: Doct: Silberrad garten.

33 Nürnbergische
Hesperides
*Johann Christoph Volckamer
(1644–1720)
Nuremberg, 1708
The growing of citrus fruit
in northern Europe
necessitated an orangery and
so presupposed considerable
wealth on the part of those
willing to engage in it.
Volckamer was one of the
first in Germany to grow
citrus fruit. A number of
different artists was
employed to work on this
book, including the
Nuremberg engraver Paul
Decker the elder, C F
Krieger and L Glotsch.*

33

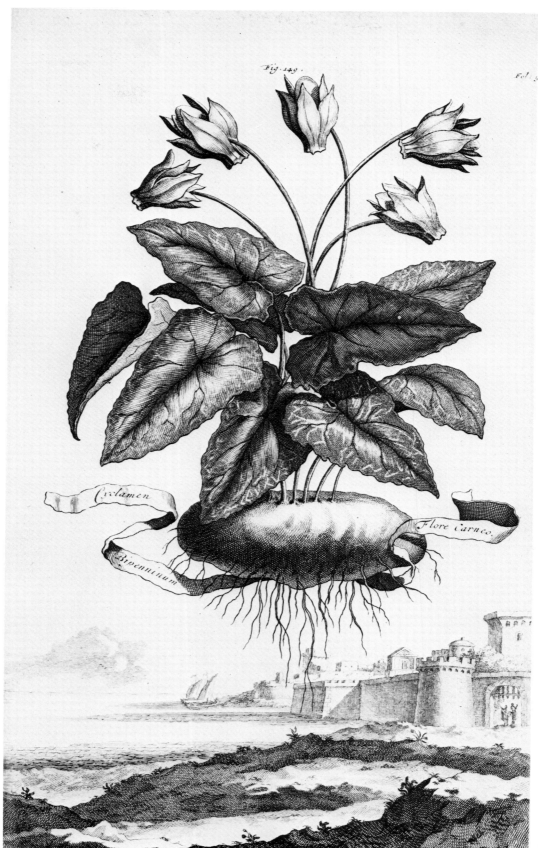

34 Naauwkeurige
Beschryving der
Aardgewassen
Abraham Munting (1626–
83)
Leyden & Utrecht: Van de
Aa & Franc. Halma, 1696
Munting was professor of
botany and chemistry in
Groningen. His book was
published posthumously and
contains illustrations by Jan
Goeree, engraved by Jan
Baptist.

34

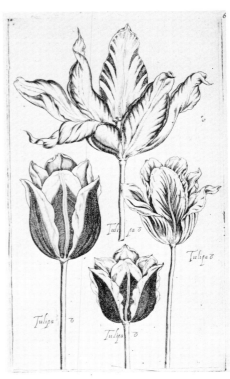

35, 36 Le jardin du roy très chrestien Loys XIII
Pierre Vallet (born c. 1575)
Paris, 1623
Vallet described himself as 'brodeur ordinaire du roi' and had published his first florilegium in 1608. Both it and the two later editions were intended as embroidery pattern books for Marie de Medici and the ladies of the court. Drawings and etchings are by Vallet. An architectural title-page leads the reader into a formal, trellised garden. The architecture is heavy and the garden beyond looks dull – very different from the title-page in Parkinson's Paradisi.

Clematis peregrina flore purpureo multiplici.

Clematis peregrina flore simplici atropurpurante.

Clematis pannonica

Clematis peregrina flore violaceo simplici.

37, 38 Theatrum Florae
Daniel Rabel (1578–1637)
3 ed. Paris: Mariette, 1633
A similar work to that by Pierre Vallet, this was first published anonymously in 1622. Rabel also worked on designs for ballet, on portraits and landscapes.

38

LE BASSIN DE LATONE, est scitue audessous du parterre d'Eau dans la demy-lune, ou Fer à cheval, trois figures de marbre blanc qui sont au milieu represente Latone et ses enfans: Les Paysans changez en Grenouilles, sont representez de differentes figures de bronze doré aussi bien que 24 Grenouilles qui sont sur le bord du bassin, Il y a au deux côtez deux autres bassins ou sont des Paysans aussi changez en Grenouilles, et autour de ces bassins des Lezards et des Tortues, le tout de bronze doré.

Perelle fecit   A Paris Chez I Mariette   rue St Jacques a la Victoire   avec privil.

39

Fait par Perelle

Veuë du Chasteau de Versaille du côté du Parterre d'Eau

A Paris Chez I. Mariette   rue S. Jacques a la Victoire. Avec Privilege du Roy

40

Receuil des plus belles maisons royales
de France

Gabriel Perelle (1603–77)

Paris: I. Mariette, 16?

Gabriel Perelle was one of a French family of painters and topographical engravers of the seventeenth and eighteenth centuries, and was a pupil of Daniel Robert and Simon Vouet. He specialized in views of Paris and Versailles.

39 In the foreground are the steps built by Le Nôtre in 1666 leading from the palace of Versailles and the 'parterre d'eau' to the Latona fountain and the parterre. The view stretches as far as the eye can see.

40 A view of the palace of Versailles from the 'parterre d'eau'. The design of this part of the gardens was changed three or four times between 1664 and 1683.

41, 42 At Chantilly the River Nonette was re-routed by Le Nôtre to create the effect he desired with the Grand Parterre to the left of the palace in Perelle's engraving.

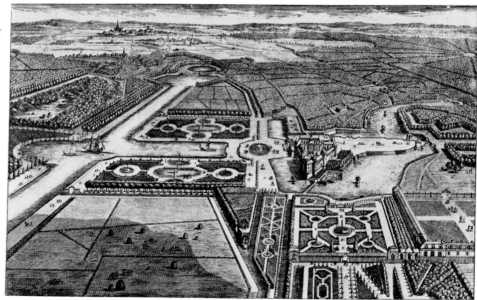

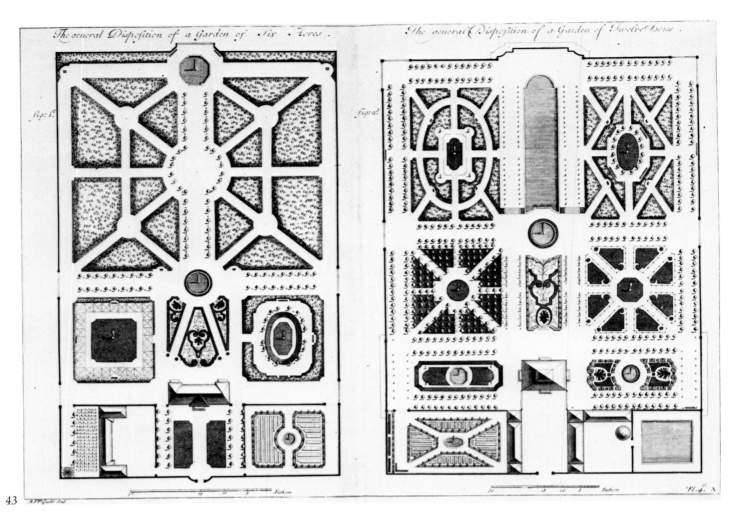

The general Disposition of a Garden of Six Acres.

The general Disposition of a Garden of Twelve Acres.

fig: 1

fig: 2

Fathom

Fathom

Pl. 4. N

43

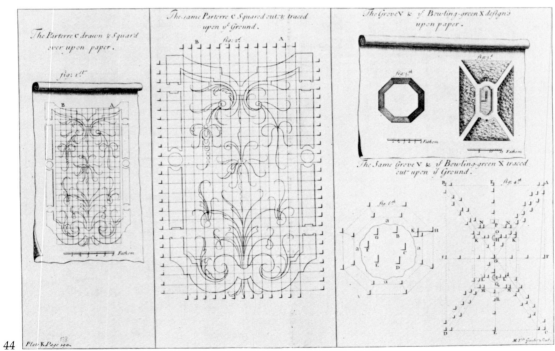

The Parterre C drawn & Squar'd over upon paper.

The same Parterre C Squared out & traced upon y⁺ Ground.

The Grove V & y⁺ Bowling-green X design'd upon paper.

fig: 1st

fig: 2d

fig: 3d

fig: 4th

The Same Grove V & y⁺ Bowling-green X traced out upon y⁺ Ground.

fig: 4th

fig: 6th

Fathom

Fathom

Fathom

44

Regum æquabat opes animis:— —.
Vir: Geor: Lib. 4: ver: 132.

THE RETIR'D GARD'NER.

The SECOND VOLUME.

Containing the Manner of

Planting and Cultivating

All Sorts of

Flowers, Plants, Shrubs, and

Under-Shrubs,

Neceſſary for the

Adorning of GARDENS:

In which is Explain'd,
The Art of Making and Diſpoſing of Parterres,
Arbours of Greens, Wood-Works, Arches, Columns, and other Pieces and Compartments uſually
found in the moſt Beautiful GARDENS of Coun-
try-Seats. The whole enrich'd with Variety of Figures, being a Tranſlation from the Sieur *Louis Liger.*

To this Volume is added, A Deſcription and Plan of
Count TALLARD's Garden at *Nottingham.*

The whole Revis'd, with ſeveral Alterations and Additions,
Which render it proper for our *Engliſh* Culture.

By *George London*, and *Henry Wiſe.*

LONDON: Printed for *Jacob Tonſon,* within
Grays-Inn Gate next *Grays-Inn* Lane. 1706.

45

**43, 44 Theory and Practice of
Gardening**
John James (? –1746)
London: Atkins, 1712
*This was the translation of A J Dezallier
d'Argenville's* La Théorie et la Pratique du
Jardinage, *which had been published in
Paris in 1709 and which did much to
popularize the ideas of Le Nôtre in
England. D'Argenville adapted Le Nôtre's
designs to gardens of smaller size. In this
plate designs for gardens of six and twelve
acres are shown. John James was an architect
who succeeded Hawksmoor as clerk of works
at Greenwich and who worked under, among
others, Wren and Vanbrugh.*

45 The Retir'd Gard'ner
*George London (? –1714) and Henry Wise
(1653–1738) Vol II. London: Tonson, 1706*
*Having already collaborated on the
publication of the English version – The
compleat gard'ner – of Jean de la
Quintinye's* Instruction pour les jardins
fruitiers *which John Evelyn had translated,
London and Wise published* The Retir'd
Gard'ner *in 1706. The work is in two*

*volumes. The first contains the English
edition, revised by London and Wise, of
François Gentil's* Le jardinier solitaire *and
the beginning of Louis Liger's* Le jardinier
fleuriste, *which is continued in the second
volume. The title-page shown here is by
Louis Laguerre and engraved by Michael van
der Gucht, who had also engraved many
plates in John James's* Theory and practice
of Gardening.

Exiguus spatio, variis sed fertilis herbis.

Engrav'd by Edward Fletcher London

46

PULSATILLA FLORE
OBSOLETO, CAULE NUDO.

Q 2

46   Catalogus Plantarum
Society of Gardeners
London, 1730
This catalogue was published by the Society
six years after its foundation to publicize
new plants introduced by members and to
clarify, as far as was possible, the
nomenclature of plants. Four volumes were
originally planned, but only this one was
published. Many famous nurserymen and
horticulturists were among the twenty
members of the Society. The title-page is
engraved by Henry Fletcher in mezzotint.
Fletcher and Elisha Kirkall engraved most of
the other plates in the Catalogus after
drawings by Jacob van Huysum. The
engravings were printed using both green
and blue, with some hand-colouring.

**47, 48   Exoticarum Aliarumque Minus
Cognitarum Plantarum**
Jacobus Breynius (1637–1697)
Danzig: D.-F. Rhetius, 1678
This fine allegorical title-page shows the
'fathers' of gardening: Solomon,
Theophrastus, Dioscorides, Pliny and Cyrus.
(Solomon was included among them because
of his supposed authorship of Ecclesiastes,
2:4–6, and the Song of Solomon;
Theophrastus, born in c. 372 BC, wrote two
large and important botanical treatises De
Historia Plantarum and De Causis
Plantarum; Dioscorides, a Greek medical
man who flourished c. AD 50, was the first
to establish medical botany as an applied

48

science; his most important work was De
Materia Medica, which remained one of the
principal botanical works for many centuries.
Pliny the Elder was a contemporary of
Dioscorides, and his Historia Naturalis was
the other basic botanical text to appear in the
first century. Finally, Cyrus the Younger,
son of Darius, king of Persia, was known to

have owned a large garden or park, which he
himself had helped to create, at Celenae. It
was the basis of Sir Thomas Browne's
seventeenth-century conceit, The Garden of
Cyrus.) The title-page is engraved by
Lambert Visscher after Andreas Stech, who
was also responsible for the drawing of the
very symmetrical 'Pulsatilla'.

49

Ex Typographia P.et I.BLAEV. Proſtant apud Viduam A.van SOMEREN. 1701.

49, 50 Horti Medici Amstelodamensis
Jan Commelin (16?–1692)
Amsterdam: P and J Blaeu, 1697–1701
Commelin was the director of the
Amsterdam physic garden, which he
managed to turn into one of the best in
Europe. Through his connections with East
India Company merchants and other
influential people he obtained plants from
overseas. The original watercolours for this
work were mostly executed by Johann and
Maria Moninckx. The engravers are
unknown. The title-page shows some very
early glasshouses.

TAB. X

TURNERA e petiolo florens, foliis ferratis. *Hort. Cliff.* 112. *ſp* 1.

1. *Ramus.*
2. *Folium ad cujus baſin duæ glandulæ. Pedunculus e petiolo enatus cum calyce fructus, ſemine, ſtylis, ſtigmatibus.*

G. D. EHRET del.

J. WANDELAAR fecit.

51 Hortus Cliffortianus
Carlus Linnaeus (1707–1778)
Amsterdam: 1737 (1738)
Linnaeus and the great botanical artist Georg Dionysius Ehret (1708–70) met at the house of George Cliffort near Haarlem in Holland. Linnaeus was writing descriptions of the rare plants in Cliffort's garden and Ehret provided the drawings. The engravings are by Jan Wandelaar, and show not only the whole stem of a plant elegantly placed upon the page, but also botanical details.

Plate XIX.

Views of Ruins after the old Roman manner for the Termination of Walks, Avenues, &c.

52

(64)

OF

GARDENS.

BOOK II.
Of TREES.

GROVES next, and well-rang'd Trees mỹ
Muſe invite,
Groves ever pleaſe, but moſt when plac'd a'right.
Without a Shade no Beauty Gardens know,
And all the Countrey's but a naked Show.

52 Le jardinier françois
RDCDWBDN (Nicolas de Bonnefons)
5 ed. Amsterdam: Jean Blaeu, 1654
This work first appeared in Paris in 1651.
The English edition was translated by John
Evelyn and was his first horticultural
publication. The engravings are by François
Chauveau, the seventeenth-century French
artist who turned from painting miniatures
to engraving.

53 New Principles of Gardening
Batty Langley (1696–1751)
London: Bettesworth, Batley & Pemberton,
1728 (1727)
Langley was a professional gardener and an
architectural writer. He advocated the 'rural
manner' in the design of gardens, and the
construction of ruins 'for the Termination of
Walks'.

54, 55 Rapin: of Gardens A Latin
Poem
James Gardiner (1679?–1732)
3 ed. London: Bernard Lintot, 1728
The original Latin poem was by the Jesuit
René Rapin (1621–87). It was published in

1665 and entitled Hortorum libri quattuor.
It was written in praise of the formal
garden. The engravings, which were first
used to illustrate the second edition of 1718,
are by Elisha Kirkall after drawings by Louis

Cheron. The headpiece is by Francis
Hoffman, whose initials are visible on the
lower right-hand side. This headpiece was
used in a number of other gardening books
published in the eighteenth century.

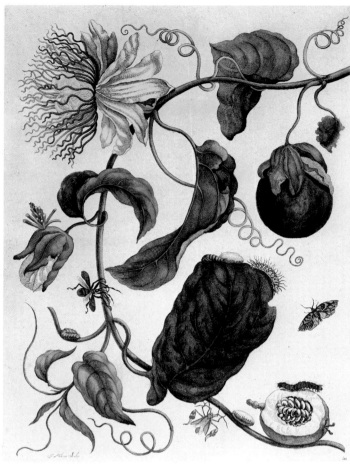

57

56, 57, 58   Over de Voortteeling en
Wonderbaerlyke Veranderingen der
Surinaamsche Insecten
Maria Sibylla Merian (1647–1717)
Amsterdam: J. F. Bernard, 1730
This work was first published in 1705.
Maria Sibylla Merian was first and foremost
an entomologist, but her flower illustrations
also put her among the leading botanical
artists of her time. The hand-coloured
engravings shown here are by Joseph Mulder
(the passion-flower) and Jan Sluyter (the
solanum).

58

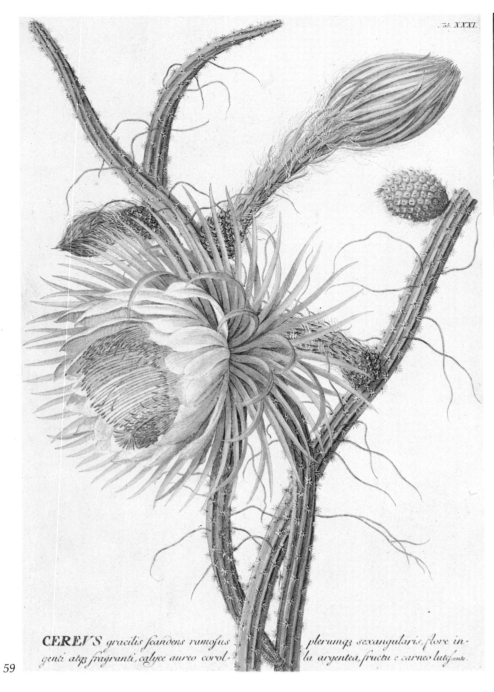

Tab. XXXI.

CEREUS *gracilis scandens ramosus plerumq3 sexangularis, flore in-*
genti atq3 fragranti, calyce aureo corol- *la argentea, fructu e carneo lutescente.*

59

6

59, 60, 61 Plantae Selectae
Christoph Jakob Trew (1695–1769)
Augsburg, 1750–73
The Nuremberg doctor Christoph Jakob Trew
had recognized the talent of Georg Dionysius
Ehret very early in his career and had
commissioned drawings from him. Wherever
Ehret was working, he sent his plant
drawings to his patron, who published them
in serial form. The engravers were Johann
Jakob Haid and his son Johann Elias. The
portrait of Ehret is a mezzotint by the elder
Haid after A. Heckell.

Tab. XI.

LILIVM *folius sparsis,* *multiflorum, floribus reflexis,*
fundo aureo, limbo auran- *tio, punctis nigricantibus,*
pedunculis singulis *unico folio instructis.*

61

Pl. 6

MIMOSA *Campeachiana.* — *Campeachy horned Mimosa.*

62, 63, 64   Figures of . . . Plants
Described in the Gardeners' Dictionary
Philip Miller (1691–1771)
3 ed. London, 1809
*The first edition of this work was published
between 1755 and 1760. The drawings are
by various artists, including John Miller and
Georg Dionysius Ehret (mimosa). Miller's
Gardeners' Dictionary was first published
in 1731 – long before the illustrations – and
was so popular that it ran to many editions
in England and abroad.*

Mesembryanthemum Caninatum

Phlox Reptans

65, 66, 67, 68 Jardin de la Malmaison
Etienne Pierre Ventenat (1757–1808)
Paris: Crapelet, 1803–5
When Malmaison became the home of the
Empress Josephine in 1798, she employed
Ventenat as her botanist and Pierre Joseph
Redouté (1759–1840) as the artist to record
the plants in her gardens. Redouté used
stipple engravings combined with colour
printing from a single plate. He successfully
defended a claim to have invented this
process in the courts. The engravers of the
four plates shown are Renard (hibiscus),
Bentely (phlox) and L. J. Allais (lavatera
and mesembryanthemum).

66

Lavatera Phoenicia

Helonias Heterophylla

69 Collection des fleurs et des fruits
peints d'après nature
Jean Louis Prévost (c. 1760 – after 1810)
Paris: Chassaignon, 1805
Prévost's work was intended more as a
pattern book than as a botanical work. The
engraver was a pupil of Francesco
Bartolozzi, Louis Charles Ruotte who
specialized in stipple engraving and colour
printing.

J.L.Prevost pinx.   A Paris chez Vilquin, M.d d'Estampes, grande cour du Palais du Tribunat. N°.20.   Ruotte sculp.

Erica Sebana

70

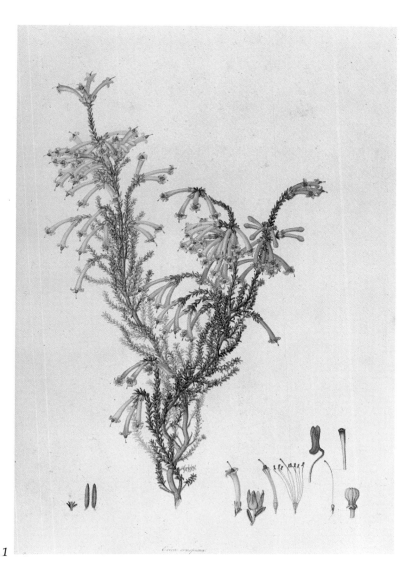

1

72

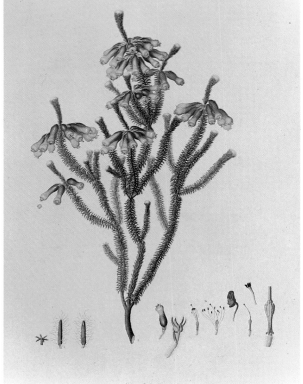

73

70, 71, 72, 73   Delineations of Exotick
Plants Cultivated in the Royal Garden at
Kew
Franz Andreas Bauer (1758–1840)
London: W. T. Aiton, 1796–1803
Franz and Ferdinand Bauer were botanical
artists from Germany who came to live in
England. Franz Bauer worked for most of
his life as an artist at Kew Gardens, at the
instigation of Sir Joseph Banks. The 'exotick
plants' are South African ericas. Most of
Bauer's water-colours were engraved by
Daniel Mackenzie, who had also been
employed by Banks to work on the plant
engravings resulting from Captain Cook's
first voyage.

CRINUM PEDUNCULATUM.

1. PAPILIO ANTENOR. 2. PAPILIO MENELAUS.

74, 75, 76, 77, 78 Selection of
Hexandrian Plants
Mrs Edward Bury (fl. 1831–37)
London: R Havell, 1831–34
Robert Havell, who also engraved Audubon's
Birds of America, *was responsible for the*
aquatints of Mrs Bury's illustrations. They
are partly printed in colour and partly hand-
coloured.

75

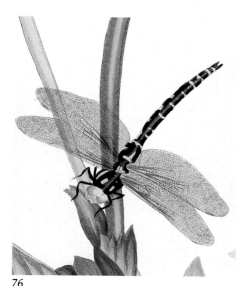

76

77

78

ILLUSTRATIONS
of
HIMALAYAN PLANTS

CHIEFLY SELECTED FROM DRAWINGS MADE FOR THE LATE

J. F. Cathcart Esqr

of the Bengal Civil Service.

THE DESCRIPTIONS AND ANALYSES BY

J. D. HOOKER M.D. F.R.S.

THE PLATES EXECUTED BY

W.H.FITCH.

79

79, 80 Illustrations of Himalayan Plants
Sir Joseph Dalton Hooker (1817–1911)
London: Reeve, 1855
J D Hooker, son of Sir William Hooker, the
Director of Kew Gardens, was a great
botanical explorer, and this book was one of

Plate II

I.D.Hld. W.Fitch lith.

Vincent Brooks imp.

HODGSONIA HETEROCLITA, Hook.fil.et Thms.

FEMALE PLANT.

two which resulted from his travels in the eastern Himalayas. The lithographs were by Walter Hood Fitch (1817–92) and were adaptations of drawings by Indian artists. Fitch, who worked for both Hookers, was a very prolific and expert botanical artist and lithographed his own work.

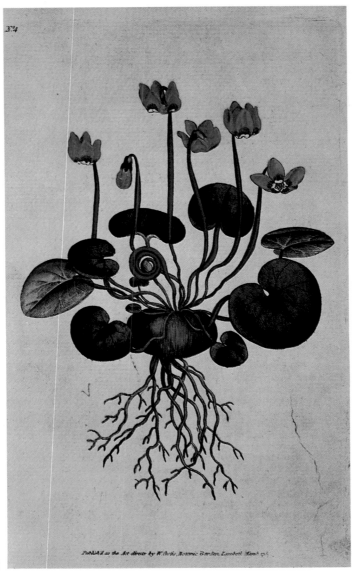

Publish'd as the Act directs by W. Curtis, Botanic Garden, Lambeth March 1787.

81

Publish'd as the Act directs by W. Curtis, Botanic Garden, Lambeth March 1787.

81, 82; 83, 84 The Botanical Magazine
*Founded by William Curtis (1746–99)
London, 1787–(still current)*

*This was the first and most successful of all
botanical magazines. The drawings and
engravings for many of the plates in the*

J. Sowerby del. et sculp.   Publish'd by W. Curtis Botanic Garden Lambeth Marsh.

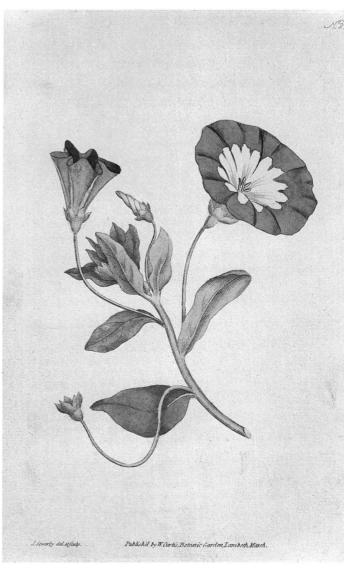

earliest volumes were by James Sowerby who signed most, but not all, of them. The plates were hand-coloured. William Curtis started life as an apothecary, but turned to botanical studies with such success that he was put in charge of the Society of Apothecaries' Physic Garden in Chelsea.

Sept. 1 1798 Published by J. Sowerby London.

85 Flora Londinensis
William Curtis (1746–99)
London, 1777–98
This was also a serial publication by Curtis,
and one which he preferred to his Botanical
Magazine. However, it was less successful
financially and was never finished. Only
seventy-two numbers with six plates and
text in each were published. Most of the
plates are unsigned but William Kilburn,
James Sowerby and Sydenham Edwards all
worked on the Flora *at some time.*

James Sowerby (1757–1822)
London, 1790–1814
Having worked for Curtis, Sowerby
eventually founded his own magazine and
was responsible for most of the illustrations,
with James Edward Smith responsible for the
text.

Convolvulus Sepium.

Hypoxis stellatta

87

87 The Botanist's Repository
Henry C. Andrews (fl. 1794–1830)
London, 1797–1812
Andrews's periodical was a rival to Curtis's
Botanical Magazine. *Its illustrations*
showed many new plants; frequently these
are described by John Kennedy, a
nurseryman who became Andrews's son-in-
law.

88 The Botanic Garden
Benjamin Maund (1790–1863)
London, 1825–51
Maund was a printer, publisher and
bookseller, and also a chemist with a passion
for flowers and gardening. Many of the
drawings for the plates were by E D Smith,
though Mrs Bury and members of Maund's
own family were also involved.

Verbena pulchella.

Iris variegata.

Antirrhinum majus.

Calendula pluvialis.

WATER AT WENTWORTH, YORKSHIRE.

89

WATER AT WENTWORTH, YORKSHIRE.

90

89, 90   Observations on the Theory and
Practice of Landscape Gardening
Humphry Repton (1752–1818)
London: Taylor, 1803
The colour plate with one of Repton's 'slides'
*(flaps) shows the estate at Wentworth in
Yorkshire before (89) and after (90) his
improvements. It is an aquatint of his
original watercolour for the Red Book
prepared for the owners of Wentworth.*

Large Flowering Sensitive Plant

91, The Temple of Flora
Robert John Thornton (1768–1837)
London, 1799–1807

This work forms the third part of Thornton's
New Illustration of the Sexual System of
Linnaeus. *Thornton employed the best*

artists for this enterprise, which was
published in serial form, but which fell
victim to the Napoleonic wars, leaving
Thornton bankrupt. It is a florilegium, but a
very romantically conceived one. The 'Large
Flowering Sensitive Plant' was painted by

Philip Reinagle and engraved in aquatint by
J C Stadler.

Henderson pinx.   *Burke & Lewis sculp.*

The Sacred Egyptian Bean

London. Published Dec.¹ 1.1804. by D.ʳ Thornton

92

RETURN OF HAPPINESS.

LILY OF THE VALLEY.

SWEET flower o' the valley, wi' blossoms of snow,
    And green leaves that turn the cauld blast frae
       their stems ;
Bright emblem o' innocence, thy beauties I lo'e,
    Aboon the king's coronet circled wi' gems !

There's no tinsel about thee; to make thee mair
       bright,
    Sweet lily ! thy loveliness a' is thine ain,
And thy bonny bells, danglin' sae pure and sae light,
    Proclaim thee the fairest o' Flora's bright train.

    This lowly plant loves the shelter of the
hollow valleys, the shade of oaks, or the cool
banks of streams.

The lily, screened from every ruder gale,
Courts not the cultured spot where roses spring.

OGILVIE.

    In the earliest days of May its snowy flowers
expand themselves, and scatter their perfume in
the air. Barton says,

        The lily, whose sweet beauties seem
        As if they must be sought.

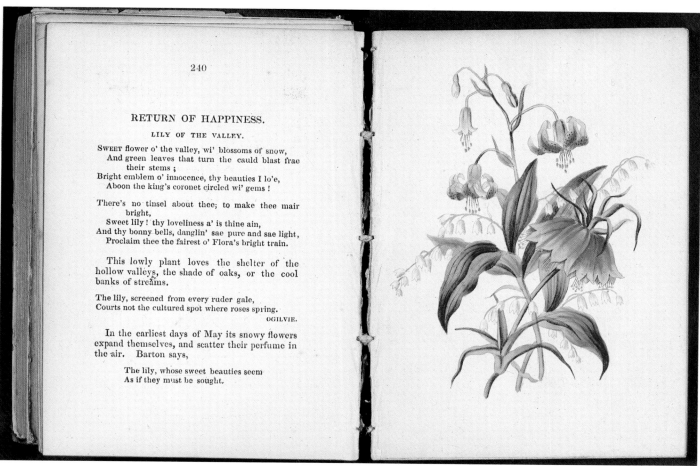

93

92   The Temple of Flora
Robert John Thornton (1768–1837)
London, 1799–1807

*The 'Sacred Egyptian Bean' was painted by
Peter Henderson and engraved by Thomas
Burke and F C Lewis. Every process of
engraving known at the time was used on
the different plates in this work.*

93   The Sentiment of Flowers
Robert Tyas
2 ed. London: Tilt, 1837
*The idea of linking flowers with a wide
variety of sentiments was very popular in
the nineteenth century. Robert Tyas, a
clergyman, produced a number of flower
books, most of them being illustrated by
James Edwards. The* Sentiment of Flowers
*was the first work on which the two men
collaborated.*

PL. 15.

1. *Linum usitatissimum* — 2. *Linum Berendieri* — 3. *Malesherbia coronata.*
4. *Malesherbia linearifolia* — 5. *Cleome pentaphylla* — 6. *Cleome spinosa*
7. *Helianthemum guttatum*

Day & Haghe Lith.rs to the Queen.

94

94, 95   The Ladies Flower Garden of
Ornamental Annuals
Jane W Loudon·(1807–1858)
London: Smith, 1842
Jane Loudon was the wife of the eminent
landscape gardener and prolific horticultural

1. *Convolvulus elongatus.* — 2. *Convolvulus tricolor.* 3. *Ipomœa bona-nox.* — 4. *Convolvulus siculus.*
5. *Ipomœa barbigera.* 6. *Convolvulus purpureus var. elatior.* 7. *Ipomœa rubra cœrulea.* 8. *Convolvulus involucratus.*
9. *Ipomœa coccinea.* — 10. *Ipomœa Quamloclit.*

Day & Haghe, Lith.rs to the Queen

writer John Claudius Loudon. Both wrote
more for the suburban villa-owners than for
the landed gentry as Capability Brown and
Humphry Repton had done. This work is
lithographed by Day and Haghe and is
partly hand-coloured.

Alstræmeria ligtu.

96

N° 57.

G. Loddiges delt.   Calendula graminifolia.   G. Cooke sc.

97

96, 97   The Botanical Cabinet
Conrad Loddiges & Sons
Vol I. London, 1817

This was more a nurseryman's catalogue
(Loddiges was a nurseryman in Hackney)
than a periodical, though it ran to twenty
volumes with a hundred plates in each. The
text and most of the drawings were the
responsibility of George Loddiges, the eldest
son. The remaining drawings and all the
engravings were by George Cooke.

98 Flora Conspicua, *Richard Morris,*
London, 1830
William Clark was responsible for the
illustrations in this work. In Mrs Hey's
Moral of Flowers *he is described as the*
'former draughtsman and engraver to the
London Horticultural Society'.

Pl. 55.

2

Drawn & Engraved by W. Clark.

London, Published by Longman & Co. Paternoster Row, Aug.t 1826.

99

99, 100, 102   The Moral of Flowers
Rebecca Hey
MS, 1831
*In 1974 the Library of the Victoria and
Albert Museum had the good fortune to be
given the manuscript and original drawings
by William Clark for this work. For the
printed version Clark prepared the
engravings from his own drawings. Rebecca
Hey compiled the verse, but, being an
excellent botanical artist who specialized in
trees, she was responsible for the
illustrations in her* Spirit of the Woods, *the
MS for which is now also in the Library.*

102

101, 103 Albums of Original Flower
Paintings
c. 1830–1855
At the same time as the gift of the two
manuscripts by Rebecca Hey was made to
the Library, the donor, Miss Janet Milne,
also gave five albums of original flower
paintings compiled and annotated by Harriet
Roberts. These paintings are by various
hands including the compiler, Rebecca Hey,
William Clark and Miss Harrison, whose
work we see here.

Index

Her Majesty's Stationery Office
Government Bookshops

49 High Holborn, London WC1V 6HB
13a Castle Street, Edinburgh EH2 3AR
41 The Hayes, Cardiff CF1 1JW
Brazennose Street, Manchester M60 8AS
Southey House, Wine Street, Bristol BS1 2BQ
258 Broad Street, Birmingham B1 2HE
80 Chichester Street, Belfast BT1 4JY

Government publications are also available
through booksellers

A full range of Museum publications
is displayed and sold at the
Victoria and Albert Museum
South Kensington
London SW7 2RL

ISBN 0 11 290375 4* cased edition

ISBN 0 11 290331 2 limp edition

Printed in England for Her Majesty's Stationery Office by W S Cowell, Ipswich